AF328228

# THE STRESS-FREE GUIDE TO POSITIVE PARENTING

EFFECTIVE STRATEGIES TO BALANCE WORK, RAISE CONFIDENT KIDS, AND BECOME THE PARENT YOUR KIDS ADORE

VINCE RODGERS LEE

# Table of Contents

# Preface

"*Parenting is easy," said no one ever.*

Let's face it—parenting while working full-time is like trying to send an email while riding a rollercoaster.

Possible? Sure.

Frustrating? Absolutely.

Perfect? Never.

Let me start by saying this—I get it. As a working parent, I've had my fair share of cold coffee mornings, Zoom calls interrupted by tiny hands waving in the background, and dinner table negotiations that rival UN peace talks. If you're reading this, chances are you've been there too.

**Why did I write this book?** It's because I've been where you are. I know the struggle of trying to do it all. I've felt the weight of wanting to be the best parent possible while also being a person with dreams and goals.

This book wasn't written from some high, untouchable mountain of perfect parenting wisdom. Nope, it was written from the trenches—between deadlines, school pick-ups, and a kid who thought the couch was a trampoline. Like you, I've tried to figure out how to balance work, life, and family without losing my mind.

My passion is to help you face these challenges and create a harmonious home. I've poured my heart into this book, drawing from my own experiences. I've written this piece with the lessons I've learned along the way.

So, grab your coffee (hopefully still warm), sit back (if you can), and let's dive in. Together, we'll figure out how to balance work, life, and parenting without losing your sanity or your sense of humor.

Welcome to *The Stress-Free Guide to Positive Parenting*. Let the adventure begin!

Vince Rodgers Lee

# Introduction

One morning, while juggling a toddler and a laptop, I realized my coffee had gone cold. Does this sound familiar? Parenting can feel like one long juggling act, with a few dropped balls and a lot of grace under pressure.

I remember my toddler asking for the millionth snack of the day while I was on a work call. My inner self was a mix of love and exhaustion. You, my dear juggling parents, are not alone.

This book is here to help you. Its purpose is simple: to offer you practical, time-efficient strategies for bringing more harmony and connection into your family life.

We all know the struggles – time is scarce, emotions run high, and sometimes you want to hide in the bathroom for a moment of peace. But here's the thing: it doesn't have to be this overwhelming. We can find calm in the chaos.

**Who is this book for?** It is for you if you're a busy new parent or a working parent trying to balance career and family. Also, it is yours if you're dealing with a house full of energy and cheekiness. You might feel like you're drowning in responsibilities, longing for more time and connection. I get it. I've been there. And that's precisely why I wrote this book.

**What makes this book special?** Yes, it's not just another parenting manual. It's full of actionable advice and real-world examples. The strategies discussed in this book aren't just theory—they're transformation. You'll find tools you can use right away and stories to make you laugh. You might see a few moments that feel like they're speaking directly to your heart.

**The book is structured to guide you step by step.** We'll start by **learning about the challenges** and **mapping out priorities**. Then, we'll move on to **establishing mindful habits** that fit into your busy life. As we move forward, we'll focus on **nurturing precious family connections**. Finally, we'll dedicate time to **refining our routines** and **celebrating the progress** we make.

And here's my call to action for you: COMMIT TO THIS JOURNEY. Embrace the process of mindful parenting. It's not about being perfect; instead, it's about being present.

Imagine a home filled with laughter, understanding, and love. That's what you hope you build, right? Well, the transformation is within your reach. And I'm here to walk alongside you every step of the way.

So, let's get started. Let's inspire and motivate each other for transformation. Take this journey with an open heart and a willing spirit. Together, we'll find the balance we all crave. Welcome to this crazy parenting adventure!

# Chapter 1

## Embarking on Your Parenting Journey

Every parent has had that moment – standing in the middle of a living room that looks like a tornado. A kid in each corner is either screaming or suspiciously quiet, and you're left wondering if you've stepped into an alternate universe. A universe where chaos is the norm.

That was me just the other day. I was trying to negotiate peace between a spat over crayons while attempting to remember if I'd sent that work email. It's a balancing act, isn't it? But here's the good news: you don't have to do it with blindfolds.

Becoming aware of your parenting style will make you feel like you've finally found the right instruction manual you've wished came with your kids. You realize that every reaction and decision somehow fits into a broader parenting philosophy. Once you know this, everything starts making more sense.

### 1.1 Discovering Your Parenting Style

Let's walk into the buffet of parenting styles, each with its own flavor. We have the **authoritative style**, which means setting clear rules but with a warm, nurturing approach. Think of it as being the loving guide on your kid's journey. You set boundaries but with a big hug.

Then there's the **permissive style**, where the motto is *"Rules are just suggestions."* This involves lots of freedom but can sometimes lead to chaos if not balanced with some structure.

We've also got the **authoritarian style**—strict, no-nonsense, and high on discipline but low on flexibility. This is the *drill sergeant approach*, which can be effective but may also stifle creativity.

Let's not forget the **uninvolved style**, which is, well, exactly what it sounds like—a bit hands-off and distant. This might not be the best recipe for connection. Knowing where you fall on this spectrum helps you make consistent and effective decisions—decisions that breed a more harmonious family dynamic.

Now, **how do you uncover your parenting style?** You should start with some **self-reflection**. You can grab a journal, sit in a quiet corner (if you can find one), and jot down your thoughts on a few prompts. It could be:

- What are the top three values you want to instill in your children?
- How do you typically handle a meltdown?
- What do you wish your parents had done differently with you?

These questions can help you see patterns in your parenting approach. There are also fun self-assessment quizzes online that can provide insights into your parenting personality. They're like those silly BuzzFeed quizzes but with a little more depth and a lot more relevance.

You should note that each style has its strengths and challenges. So, knowing them can help you quickly pull through the ups and downs of parenting. For example, authoritative parents often see higher success in instilling independence and self-discipline in their kids. Permissive parents might excel at nurturing creativity and individuality.

However, permissive parents might struggle with setting boundaries, while authoritarian parents may suffer constant power struggles. Case studies abound, showcasing real-life scenarios of families thriving under each style. They offer a wealth of lessons for you to consider.

But here's the kicker: parenting is not a one-size-fits-all endeavor. It's a dynamic, evolving process, much like the children we raise. Kids grow, and so do we. The key is adaptability – being open to tweaking your approach as your children's needs and personalities develop.

Perhaps your toddler's boundless curiosity calls for more structure today, while your teenager might thrive under a bit more freedom tomorrow. Flexibility is your best friend on this journey. It allows you to adjust and grow alongside your children.

As they say, ***change is the only constant thing.*** And, that's especially true in parenting. So, embrace the flow, and remember that no style is set in stone.

## 1.2 Ways to Identify Emotional Triggers

Let's say you're in the grocery store with a list and a toddler who's just seen the candy aisle. Suddenly, a meltdown ensues, and you can feel your blood pressure rising along with the stares of fellow shoppers. What just happened?

Say hello to **emotional triggers**. These are those hidden buttons that, when pressed, can turn a calm parent into a mess. Knowing these triggers can affect how we interact with our children. We might be able to avoid negative reactions that surprise even us. Recognizing these triggers can help us respond with more intention rather than reacting in the moment.

Every parent has unique emotional triggers. They might include:

- A child's defiance.
- Incessant whining.
- Simple messiness of everyday life, and more.

The science behind this is fascinating. Our brains are wired to react to stressors. This is a leftover from our ancient ancestors who needed to react quickly to survive. Unfortunately, this can mean that a toddler's tantrum sets off the same fight-or-flight response. Much like the response a saber-toothed tiger might have in prehistoric times.

Understanding the science of emotional responses helps us appreciate how normal yet challenging these reactions can be. But **how do we become aware of these triggers?** Well, **mindfulness** is a good place to start. It's the practice of being fully present and aware.

Mindfulness can help us identify what sets us off. Try this: when you feel that familiar rush of frustration, pause. Take a deep breath and ask yourself what's really bothering you. Is it the noise, the mess, or perhaps the fear of judgment from others?

**Daily reflection**, even if it's just a few minutes of quiet thought or jotting down your feelings, can reveal patterns. Maybe you notice you're more sensitive to defiance when you're tired or hungry. This awareness is the first step to managing these triggers.

Once we identify our triggers, we need **effective coping mechanisms**. Start with breathing exercises. They're simple but powerful. When you feel that wave of emotion, try inhaling deeply for four counts, holding for four, and exhaling for four.

**Breathing exercises** can instantly calm your nervous system, giving you a moment to choose your response. Also, **developing a personal mantra** can be helpful. Something as simple as *"This too shall pass"* or *"It's just a phase"* repeated silently can ground you in the moment. It can remind you that you have the power to choose your reaction.

Regulating our emotions doesn't just bring us peace; it transforms our home environment. When we manage our responses, we model emotional control for our children. They learn to handle their own emotions by watching us.

The positive outcomes are undeniable:

- Fewer power struggles.
- More effective communication.
- A general sense of calm permeates the household.

Imagine handling a tantrum with the grace of a *Zen master.*

It might not happen overnight, but with practice, you'll find that calm is contagious.

The real magic of emotional regulation lies in the way it changes our relationships with our children. It breeds an environment where they feel safe to express themselves. This is because they know that their parents will respond with understanding rather than anger or frustration.

Emotionally regulated parents tend to raise children who are:

- More adaptable
- Resilient
- Emotionally intelligent, and more.

So, let's embrace the messiness of parenting and remember that it's okay to have those moments. What matters is how we bounce back and grow from them.

## 1.3 Prioritizing Family Goals

Ever felt like life is a never ending cycle of to-dos? One where your dreams for family time get lost somewhere between work emails and grocery lists? Trust me, you're not alone. Setting family goals can feel like trying to herd cats while balancing a unicycle.

But here's a little secret: defining clear family goals. This can be like flipping on a GPS when you're utterly lost. It gives you direction, helps align everyone's efforts, and builds a sense of unity. This makes those everyday challenges a bit more manageable.

First, let's discuss long-term versus short-term goals. Think of **long-term goals** as the big picture—the family, which you're painting over the years. These are dreams like saving for a family vacation next year or building a home library.

**Short-term goals**, on the other hand, are the brushstrokes that get you there. They're the weekly or monthly steps. Things like setting aside a small amount from each paycheck or dedicating an evening a week to reading.

Both long-term and short-term goals are necessary. You need to align your personal values with these goals to ensure they resonate with everyone in the family. If education and creativity are high on your list, maybe your goal is to foster a love for learning through shared activities. It's all about making sure your goals reflect what truly matters to your family.

The next step is setting these goals, and this is where the **SMART framework** comes in handy. SMART stands for:

S- specific
M- measurable
A- achievable
R- relevant
T- timely.

Let's say you want more quality family time. A SMART goal would be:

*"Have a no-screen family night every Friday for the next three months."*

- It's **specific** (no screens, Friday nights)
- It's **measurable** (once a week)
- It's **achievable** (it's just one night)
- It's **relevant** (it strengthens family bonds)
- It's **timely** (for three months).

This clarity helps everyone know what they're working towards and how to get there.

Now, gather the crew for a family goal-setting meeting. These meetings are a great way to get everyone on the same page. Involve your kids by asking what they'd like to achieve. You might be surprised by their ideas. Perhaps they want to learn to cook a meal together or plan a family camping trip.

**Assign roles and responsibilities that suit each family member's strengths.** Maybe one child is in charge of picking a recipe, while another is the designated DJ for your family night. Giving everyone a role not only makes the goal more achievable but also instills a sense of accountability.

But let's not forget the importance of **reviewing and adjusting these goals.** Life happens – schedules get crazy, interests change, and that's perfectly okay. Regular family check-ins can help assess how you're doing.

Maybe the Friday night idea isn't working because of soccer practices. No problem! Shift it to Saturday, or find a new activity that works better. **Flexibility is key.** These check-ins are also a time to celebrate progress, no matter how small.

Did you manage a whole month of family nights? Awesome! Celebrate with a little family treat or outing. These moments of recognition keep motivation high. It reminds everyone why these goals matter in the first place.

In the end, prioritizing family goals doesn't mean creating a rigid plan that never changes. It's about setting a course that brings your family closer together. That way, you align your actions with your values and become open to the twists and turns along the way. It's about knowing where you're headed and enjoying the ride together.

## 1.4 How to Categorize Tasks

Let's face it, the to-do list of a parent often reads like a novel rather than a list. From work demands to school drop-offs, meal preps, and everything else squeezed in between. It's no wonder we sometimes feel like we're spinning plates while juggling flaming torches. Here's the good news: not every task is of equal importance, and that's where **categorizing tasks** comes in handy.

Think of it as triaging your daily life. To do this, you need to first identify **what's essential**. These are the tasks that, if left undone, result in chaos. They include:

- Feeding your kids
- Paying bills
- Keeping up with work commitments, etc.

They're the non-negotiables and the backbone of your routine. Without them, the whole operation could crumble.

Next, we have **tasks that are perfect candidates for delegation**. These aren't necessarily burdens, but they're not crucial for you to handle alone. Maybe it's folding laundry or organizing the pantry. It's okay to let go of the reins a bit. Involving your children in household tasks not only lightens your load but also teaches them responsibility.

A chore chart can work wonders here. For partners, a conversation about shared duties can make a big difference. Maybe your partner takes over dinner duty a couple of nights a week, freeing you up to focus on something else.

Then, the real magic is eliminating **tasks**. This requires a little introspection and honesty. Are there things you do out of habit rather than necessity? Maybe it's that weekly deep-cleaning ritual that leaves you exhausted. Or perhaps it's volunteering for every school event.

Take a moment to evaluate what truly needs your attention and what doesn't. Letting go of unnecessary tasks can be liberating. It's like clearing out a mental closet. You make space for what really matters. It could be a little time for those spontaneous dance-offs in the living room or quiet moments for a bedtime story.

## Creating Task Charts for the Family

Visual aids like task charts can transform a chaotic household into a perfect one. Create a chart that lists daily, weekly, and monthly tasks, assigning names next to each one. Use colors or stickers to make it engaging for kids.

This enforces accountability and turns hectic chores into a family project. It allows everyone to see what needs to be done and who is responsible. This makes delegation a shared responsibility rather than a top-down command.

Delegation doesn't mean offloading duties; it's about building a team mentality. You can have a heart-to-heart with your partner about the mental load, which often goes unspoken but heavily felt. Discuss what tasks can be shared or alternated.

Maybe it's taking turns with school pick-ups or meal planning.

**Communication here is key**. When everyone knows their role, the household runs smoother, and there's a greater sense of unity.

Now, let's talk about **the art of letting go.** It's not easy, but it's necessary. Ask yourself: does this task need to be done by me? Regularly evaluate your responsibilities. That is, what can you streamline or simplify? Maybe meal prep means doubling a recipe and freezing half for later. Or perhaps you decide that a tidy home is good enough and perfection is overrated.

Letting go of unnecessary tasks doesn't translate to cutting corners. Instead, it's about prioritizing joy and connection over an endless to-do list.

In recent times, it's easy to get swept up in the busyness. But by categorizing tasks, we can create space for what truly matters. We can focus on essentials, share the load, and release the rest. It's a journey towards finding balance and breathing room. That way, we can make way for laughter, love, and precious moments that make parenting joyful.

## 1.5 Setting Weekly Targets for Success

Imagine standing at the base of a mountain, looking up to the peak. It's daunting, right? But what if you could break that climb into smaller, manageable steps? Each one is a small victory on its own. That's the magic of setting weekly targets.

Instead of seeing your family goals as a gigantic, overwhelming task, break them down. **Smaller targets** make the overall goal seem less intimidating. It also provides a steady stream of successes to celebrate. These short-term victories build momentum and keep everyone motivated.

Weekly planning sessions can become a cherished family ritual. A time when everyone gathers around the table, maybe with some snacks and plans for the week ahead. This shouldn't be about doing chores or assignments alone. It should align with everyone's expectations and goals.

It's a chance to discuss what each person hopes to achieve that week. It could be a school project, a work deadline, or simply finding time to relax. By the end of the session, everyone leaves with a clear sense of what's essential and what needs to be prioritized.

To keep things on track, **create a weekly family planner**. This can be a simple calendar on the fridge or a digital app that everyone can access. The key is to have a visual representation of the week so everyone knows what's happening and when.

Encourage each family member to jot down their targets, no matter how small. Did your teen want to finish a book? Did your partner plan to tackle the garden? Document it all. At the end of the week, take a moment to reflect on what was achieved and what challenges popped up.

Then, celebrate the wins! Also, learn from the misses and adjust for the next week. It becomes an ongoing cycle of improvement and adaptation, much like life itself.

**Maintaining motivation and accountability isn't always easy**, especially when life gets hectic. But with a few strategies, it becomes manageable. Consider implementing a reward system to achieve weekly targets.

Rewards don't have to be extravagant. It could be a family movie night, choosing the menu for dinner, or a simple acknowledgment of effort can do wonders. This recognition incentivizes reaching goals and also reinforces the value of working together as a team.

Another powerful tool is the concept of **family accountability partners**. Much like a workout buddy, having someone in the family to check in with can keep everyone on track. Maybe it's a sibling pairing to see who can keep their room tidy. It could be parents checking in on each other's goals. This partnership helps create support and connection. It reminds everyone that they're part of a larger unit working toward shared objectives.

As you imbibe these practices into your routine, you'll likely notice a shift. Yes, life will still throw curveballs, and not every week will go as planned. But with weekly targets, there's a structure and rhythm to your family's days.

Each week becomes a chapter in your family's story, filled with its own challenges and triumphs. The beauty lies:

- In the process.
- In the shared journey of setting goals.
- In supporting each other.
- In celebrating how far you've come.

So, as you continue to pull through the delightful chaos of parenting, keep in mind that even the smallest steps forward are progress. Embrace the little victories, stay flexible, and remember that each week is an opportunity to grow closer as a family. The climb may be steep, but the view from the top is worth every step.

# Chapter 2

## *Intending Mindful Habit*

So, It's 7 a.m., and the house is awake, but you're not quite ready to face the day. The kids are already up, their energy levels rivaling that of a hyperactive squirrel. But you're just trying to locate your coffee mug. Sound familiar?

What if I told you that a bit of structure in the morning could transform the chaos into something that at least resembles order? A consistent morning routine isn't just about getting out of the house on time. Instead, it sets the stage for a day where you feel like you're steering the ship instead of being tossed around by the waves.

Studies show that a structured morning can uplift everyone's mood. This makes the difference between a day that starts with smiles and one that begins with stress.

Now, let's craft a personalized morning ritual that suits your unique family dynamics. Every family is different, so *cookie-cutter routines* won't do. Start by **incorporating quick breakfast rituals** that get everyone at the table, even for just ten minutes. It could be as simple as a *"toast toppings bar"* where everyone gets creative with spreads and sprinkles.

This small moment of togetherness can kickstart connection and conversation. Pair this with **morning affirmatio**ns or a **gratitude practice**. Imagine kicking off the day by sharing one thing everyone is thankful for. It's a simple practice, but it sets a positive tone and reminds everyone of what matters most.

Mindfulness isn't reserved for yoga retreats or quiet mountain tops. It's something you can sprinkle into your mornings like *magic dust*. Consider starting the day with a few minutes of meditation. It doesn't have to be a full-on session – just a moment to close your eyes, breathe deeply, and set your intentions.

If meditation feels like a chore, try **mindful stretching**. Even the kids can join in! You can turn it into a game by pretending to be different animals. Stretch like a cat, reach for the sky like a giraffe, or sway like a tree in the wind. These moments of mindfulness can warm up both you and your children. Thereby creating a more centered start to the day.

**The key to all this is consistency**. You might be thinking, "Sure, this sounds nice, but how do I actually make it happen every day?" Here's a little secret: visual aids work wonders. You can create a morning routine chart.

This chart can be as simple as a whiteboard with colorful markers or a printed chart with pictures for the little ones. Place it where everyone can see it. This serves as a gentle reminder of what comes next, reducing the need for constant verbal prompts. It also allows the morning to flow more smoothly.

Over time, these routines become second nature, a habit that feels less like a chore and more like a natural rhythm.

## 2.1 The Morning Routine Chart Template

Consider crafting your own morning routine chart.

- Grab some paper or use a digital tool to design a chart that outlines each step of the morning.
- Add pictures or icons for younger children who can't read yet.
- Below each task, leave a space for them to place a sticker or draw a smiley face once completed.

This not only visually represents progress but also instills a sense of accomplishment in completing each step. Remember, the goal isn't perfection. Some mornings will unravel no matter how well you plan, and that's okay.

**Flexibility is your ally**. We mentioned this in the first chapter. The true benefit of a mindful morning routine lies in creating a foundation that supports you and your family. It isn't about rigidly adhering to every detail.

As you experiment with these rituals, you'll discover what works best for you. Therefore, embrace the mistakes and celebrate the successes, knowing that each morning is a new opportunity to connect, grow, and start again.

## 2.2 Creating Night time Rituals for Calm

Evenings, much like mornings, can run from serene to utterly chaotic. After the whirlwind of the day, the idea of winding down might feel like a distant dream. It's worse when the kids have seemingly endless energy reserves. This means creating a peaceful evening routine is more than a luxury you should afford. It's a game-changer for your family's well-being.

Consistent bedtime rituals can significantly improve sleep quality and help everyone de-stress after a long day. When you establish a calming routine, you're whispering to your body that it's time to ease into rest mode. This makes it easier for everyone to drift off and recharge.

One of my favorite ways to wind down is through family-centered activities. You know those activities that bring everyone together in a relaxing setting? Yes! Imagine gathering the kids in the living room for a lovely storytime. It's one where you get to swap tales, whether it's a beloved bedtime story or a chapter from a favorite book.

It's more than the story. What matters is the shared experience, the cuddles, and the giggles over silly voices. For older kids, reflective journaling can be a wonderful way to end the day. Encourage them to jot down their thoughts, what they're grateful for, or even just doodles of their day. It can be a quiet moment of introspection that helps them process their experiences and relax.

Now, we all know screens can be a siren song, luring us into late-night scrolling or binge-watching. You'll agree that reducing screen time before bed is crucial for a restful night. I suggest setting up a tech-free zone at least an hour before bedtime. This might sound ambitious, but it's a powerful way to signal to your brain that it's time to slow down.

Instead of screens, bring out board games, puzzles, or even coloring books. These activities help engage everyone and create a calm, screen-free environment. It sets the body for more restful sleep. You can consider creating a family charging station where all devices are plugged in for the night. This station makes gadgets out of reach and hopefully out of mind.

To further ease the transition from a busy day to a restful night, consider incorporating mindfulness into your bedtime routine. Guided bedtime meditation can be an excellent tool for this. You don't need to be a meditation guru; there are plenty of apps and online resources that are perfect for kids and adults alike.

Just a few minutes of focusing on breathing can work wonders for melting away the day's stress. **Breathing exercises are another great option**. Try a simple technique where you breathe in for four counts. That is, hold for four, and exhale for four. It's a quick way to calm the nervous system and prepare for sleep.

It might take a little time for everyone to adjust, but stick with it. Over time, these routines become a cherished part of your family's day. It can become a time when everyone knows it's okay to let go of the day's worries and just be.

The beauty of these rituals lies in their simplicity and the way they help to build connections. In those quiet moments, as you tuck your child in, you're not just preparing for sleep. You're building memories, nurturing bonds, and creating a peaceful haven for everyone to recharge.

## 2.3 Integrating Mindfulness into Daily Tasks

Mindfulness. It's that word we hear everywhere, but what does it really mean for us busy parents? At its core, mindfulness is being present – fully engaged in the here and now without judgment. It's paying attention to our thoughts, feelings, and surroundings, but without the constant commentary running through our heads.

Imagine it as tuning into the present moment with all your senses, whether you're folding laundry or savoring a cup of tea. The beauty of mindfulness is its versatility. It can be incorporated into everyday tasks, turning the chaotic into meaningful moments.

Consider **mindful eating** during family meals. Instead of scarfing down food while scrolling through your phone, try savoring each bite. Discuss the texture or taste with your kids. Ask them where they think the ingredients came from or what flavors they can identify. This encourages healthier eating habits and also turns mealtime into a shared sensory experience.

It can be a playful way to introduce mindfulness to children, who are naturally curious to explore the world through their senses. Similarly, during the school drop-off or pick-up, practice mindful walking. Notice the rhythm of your steps, the warmth of the sun, or the coolness of the breeze. It's like a mini-vacation for your mind inside the hustle of the day.

Engaging children in mindfulness might seem like a tall order, especially when they're bouncing off the walls. However, there are creative ways to integrate it into their daily activities. For instance, **mindful coloring or drawing** can be a fantastic introduction.

Encourage them to focus on the colors they choose, the sound of the pencil on paper, or the patterns they create.

It's all about immersing them in the process rather than fixating on the end product. Another fun activity is **mindful listening games**. Sit quietly with your child and take turns identifying the sounds you hear, whether it's a bird chirping, a car passing by, or the hum of the refrigerator.

These simple activities build a sense of calm and presence. This can help children develop emotional awareness and self-regulation skills over time.

The long-term benefits of adopting a mindful lifestyle are profound. It's not just about finding moments of peace in a chaotic day; it's about transforming your entire approach to life's challenges. Parents who embrace mindfulness often report enhanced emotional regulation. They feel less reactive to stressors and enjoy improved relationships with their children.

As you practice mindfulness, you cultivate a feeling of inner calm that radiates outward. This creates a more harmonious and connected family life. It's like a ripple effect – when you're centered, you can respond to your children with more extraordinary patience and understanding. In return, they learn to mirror that calmness in their own behavior.

Mindfulness offers a way to slow down and savor life's little moments. You know those brief but precious times that might otherwise slip by unnoticed? It's like hitting the pause button on the frenetic pace of life, allowing you to fully engage with your family in the present.

Over time, these practices can:

- Reduce overall stress.
- Improve focus
- Foster a more profound sense of connection within your household, etc.

It's not just about the immediate benefits, mindfulness lays the groundwork for a more resilient and compassionate family dynamic. One where each member feels valued and heard. It's a powerful tool for nurturing empathy and understanding, both within ourselves and with those we love most.

## 2.4 Using Habit Trackers for Progress

If you're anything like me, running a zillion things while trying to remember if you replied to that email, habit tracking might just be your new best friend. Imagine having a tool that keeps you on track and also adds motivation to your day. **Habit trackers** do precisely that by making progress visible.

They transform abstract goals into tangible steps, giving you a little happy moment every time you tick a box or fill in a bubble. There's a surprising satisfaction in seeing a row of completed tasks lined up like little soldiers, each representing a victory over chaos. When the whole family gets involved, accountability turns into a shared adventure.

Setting up a habit tracker isn't rocket science, but it does require a bit of thought. Start by figuring out what works best for your family. Some people love the tactile pleasure of paper, while others prefer the convenience of digital solutions. A **family**

**habit tracking chart** can be a simple poster in the kitchen where everyone can see it.

You could opt for an app that pings reminders directly to your phone. For the tech-savvy family, apps like Joon or Habitshare can be game-changers, especially if you love a little bit of gamification. The key is to choose a method that fits your lifestyle and that everyone can access easily.

Once your tracker is up and running, the real magic happens in the weekly reviews. Take a few minutes each week to gather the family and look over what's been achieved. It's not just about patting yourself on the back, though that's definitely part of it. More importantly, it's about assessing what worked, what didn't, and why. Maybe you set a goal that was too ambitious, or perhaps a particular habit didn't fit well with your daily routine. This is your chance to tweak and adjust, ensuring that your goals remain realistic and achievable. It's a dynamic process, much like family life itself. Also, it allows everyone to feel involved and invested in the outcome.

Celebrating milestones is *the icing on the cake*, and it's necessary for keeping everyone motivated. When a family member reaches a habit goal, make it a big deal. It doesn't have to be extravagant. It can be a family movie night, a favorite meal, or even just some extra screen time, which can be enough to acknowledge the effort.

The point is to recognize and celebrate the dedication it took to reach that milestone. This not only boosts morale but also reinforces the value of persistence and teamwork. It turns habit tracking into a fun family project that everyone looks forward to.

**The benefits of habit tracking** extend beyond mere task

completion. It inculcates a sense of accomplishment and builds a positive cycle of behavior reinforcement. As you and your family see the progress you're making together, you cultivate a sense of shared purpose and achievement.

It's more than just ticking boxes; it's about building habits that support a more balanced and fulfilling family life. With each milestone, you're celebrating the completion of a task and also celebrating the small steps that lead to more significant changes. This creates a household that thrives on collaboration and mutual support.

## 2.5 Aligning Habits with Family Values

Have you ever paused to think about what truly drives your family? I mean beyond the daily hustle, the school runs, and the ever-present hunt for clean socks. It's easy to get caught up in the neverending tasks. But what about your family values? These are the guiding stars that help in making decisions – big and small.

When you align your habits with these core values, it's like you've given your family a more cohesive identity. That is, a shared purpose that resonates with everyone. A value-driven life builds a sense of belonging and strengthens bonds.

To get started, **consider sitting down as a family for a heart-to-heart discussion** about what truly matters to you. This is more than crafting a mission statement worthy of a corporate retreat. It's more than that. It's about understanding what makes your family unique.

**What do you want your kids to remember about their**

**childhood?** Is it the kindness you showed others, the respect for nature, or perhaps the dedication to hard work and perseverance? Let each family member share their thoughts.

You might be surprised by what your kids value. It could be fairness, creativity, or simply the joy of spending time together. This exercise includes listing values, prioritizing them, and understanding how they shape your family's identity.

Once you've identified your core values, it's time to reflect them in your daily habits. Think about small, actionable steps that embody these principles. If kindness and empathy are at the top of your list, make acts of kindness a daily habit. It doesn't have to be grand gestures. Sometimes, a simple smile or a helping hand speaks volumes.

If environmental consciousness is important, consider habits like recycling, conserving water, or supporting local produce. It's about making choices that align with what you hold dear and involving your children in these practices.

They learn by watching and doing, so encourage them to participate in activities that reflect their family values. It could be volunteering together, starting a compost bin, or even just talking about why you choose to walk instead of driving when possible.

Living in alignment with your values has a profound impact on family settings. It brings clarity to daily decisions and strengthens your family's unity. When everyone is on the same page, there's a sense of harmony that fills the household. You're not just coexisting under one roof; you're a team working towards a common purpose.

This shared mission enhances relationships, as each family member understands and supports the values that bind you together. When conflicts arise – and they will – you can return to these guiding principles as a way to find solutions that honor your shared beliefs.

A family that lives according to its values is like a tree with deep roots. It stands strong against the winds of change, flexible yet grounded. As you move forward, these habits will continue to evolve with you. Life is dynamic, and so are your values.

You might want to revisit them periodically, perhaps during family meetings or quiet evenings. This is to ensure that they continue to reflect who you are becoming, both individually and collectively. This ongoing reflection keeps your family's values aligned with your growth, ensuring that your habits remain relevant and meaningful.

In essence, aligning your habits with your family values enriches your daily life. It turns routine actions into intentional practices that reinforce your identity and strengthen your bonds. It's a powerful way to ensure that your family isn't just surviving but thriving. It ensures that your family is grounded in what matters most.

# Chapter 3

## *Nurturing Emotional Connections*

Imagine it's a Saturday afternoon, and somehow, you've found yourself in a rare quiet moment. The kids are off building a pillow fort or negotiating the terms of a peace treaty over the last cookie. You sip your coffee and realize, hey, maybe this parenting thing isn't so bad after all.

But then it hits you. When was the last time you genuinely connected with each of them one-on-one? Really, between work, chores, and the general chaos of life, when was the last time? The thought lingers, and you might start to see the significance of those small pockets of personal time.

Spending individual time with each child might feel like a luxury. But it's actually a cornerstone of healthy development. When we give our kids undivided attention, even for a few minutes, we're building their confidence and helping them feel valued.

It's like watering a plant. If you neglect it, it wilts; if you tend to it, it thrives. These moments of connection provide opportunities for our kids to:

- Open up.
- Share their thoughts.
- Feel truly heard.

They help children develop a strong sense of self-worth, knowing that they're important.

But let's be honest: finding time for these one-on-one moments can feel like searching for a unicorn. Life is hectic, and sometimes it seems like there aren't enough hours in the day. Still, with a few significant moves, you can make it happen.

You can start by looking at your current schedule and identifying small windows of opportunity. Maybe it's those few minutes after dinner when you're cleaning up, or it could be on the ride back from soccer practice. Make sure to use these moments to chat, listen, and engage.

Now, for some scheduling hacks, try setting a recurring "date" with each child. It doesn't have to be extravagant; just set aside a consistent time for them.

Once a week, you might have breakfast together before everyone else wakes up. You could also share a bedtime story that's just for the two of you. **The key is consistency, not quantity.** These regular interactions build connections that strengthen over time.

But when it comes to activities, you'll need to think outside the box. Crafting or cooking together can be wonderful ways to bond. Just let your child choose a recipe, and then swing into the mess and magic of creating something together.

If your little one is an outdoor person, you can plan adventures that cater to their interests. It can be a simple walk in the park, a bike ride, or even a backyard campout under the stars. The activity itself matters less than the shared experience. It's in these moments that conversations flow, and connections deepen.

The long-term benefits of these interactions are profound. By investing in these one-on-one times, you're laying the foundation for a lasting relationship—a relationship built on trust and understanding.

Your child is able to grow up feeling secure, knowing that they have a safe space with you. They carry this sense of belonging with them into the world, pulling through life's challenges with confidence.

### 3.1 The One-on-One Time Tracker

Consider using a simple tracker to ensure each child gets their special time. It can be a calendar where you mark out dedicated slots for each child. It could also be a more creative approach with tokens or stickers. The goal is to visualize and prioritize these moments amidst the hustle.

In the parenting storm, it's easy to lose sight of individual connections. Yet, these connections provide the anchor amidst the storm. They remind us and our children that we're in this together, side by side.

### 3.2 Practicing Active Listening with Empathy

You know those moments when your child is telling you about their day, and your mind is doing the mental gymnastics of tomorrow's to-do list? We've all been there, but here's where active listening comes into play.

It's more than just hearing words; it's about tuning in and showing your child that what they say matters. Active listening involves giving your full attention, making eye contact, and nodding along. It's not just because you're agreeing but because you're engaged.

It's setting aside the buzzing phone and the endless distractions to be present in that moment. This kind of listening created trust and understanding. It builds a safe space for your child to express themselves without fear of judgment or dismissal.

Communication is like a dance, and active listening ensures you're not stepping on each other's toes. One effective strategy is paraphrasing. That is, repeating back what your child says, not like a parrot, but like a mirror reflecting their thoughts and feelings. It shows them they are heard and valued.

*"So, you felt left out when your friends didn't invite you to play?"*

This simple act can open the floodgates of communication, inviting them to share more. Asking open-ended questions is another powerful tool.

Instead of *"Did you have a good day?"* try *"What was the best part of your day?"*

It invites more than a yes or no and encourages deeper reflection. This approach improves communication and strengthens the relationship. It makes it easier for your child to come to you with their hopes and troubles as they grow.

Note also that empathy plays a starring role in effective communication. It's about walking in your child's shoes and trying to understand their world from their perspective. When you acknowledge and validate their emotions, you teach them that feelings are okay and that they're not alone in experiencing them.

Empathy then becomes a tool for conflict resolution, helping you sail through the stormy seas of tantrums and teenage rebellion. It's saying:

*"I see you're really upset about this, and it's okay to feel that way."*

By validating their emotions, you help them learn to manage and express their feelings healthily. You want to build resilience and emotional intelligence.

Of course, active listening comes with its own set of hurdles. Life is filled with distractions, from the ping of text messages to the never-ending list of chores. But there are ways to overcome these barriers.

**Try creating a dedicated space for conversations**, free from screens and noise. Even if it's just the dinner table, make it a tech-free zone where everyone can talk and listen without interruption. It's about setting boundaries and creating an environment conducive to authentic connection.

Sometimes, just getting down to their level—literally—can make a difference. Sitting eye-to-eye can help your child feel more comfortable opening up because they have your undivided attention.

Active listening and empathy are like gifts you give each other. They build a bridge of understanding and trust that can weather the storms of a child's upbringing. This type of connection is the glue that holds families together.

You'll want to build a sense of belonging and security. As you practice, it will become second nature, an effortless dance. This will bring you closer to your children and teach them by example how to be compassionate communicators.

## 3.3 Celebrating Family Wins with Creativity

We'll all know that a small pat on the back can light up a kid's face like a Christmas tree. Therefore, celebrating family achievements is a bit like sprinkling magic dust over everyday life.

Acknowledging successes, no matter how tiny, strengthens the bonds within the family. It boosts morale, creating an environment where everyone feels appreciated. When you celebrate achievements, you're marking an accomplishment and reinforcing the idea that effort is worth acknowledging.

This can be as simple as a *"Well done!"* for completed homework or a "*High-five*" for brushing your teeth without a fuss. What you're doing is recognizing both the big and small victories that make up family life.

Now, let's talk about getting creative with celebrations. Think outside the box and make it an event to remember. How about hosting a DIY family awards night? Imagine a red carpet made of old bedsheets. Each family member can receive a handmade trophy for something unique they've achieved.

Perhaps *"Best Lego Builder"* or *"Most Creative Pancake Maker."* These little accolades can become treasured memories. It can spark joy and laughter. You can consider creating a family success scrapbook.

Fill the scrapbook with photos, notes, and mementos from your family's achievements. This provides a tangible record of accomplishments, and flipping through its pages can be a comforting reminder of what you've achieved together.

Celebrations aren't just fun; they serve as powerful positive reinforcement. They encourage continued effort and cooperation by creating a culture of encouragement and support. When children know that their hard work will be recognized, they're more motivated to keep trying.

You're building an environment where everyone feels that their contributions matter. Think of it as planting seeds of positivity that will grow into resilience. Positive reinforcement doesn't just benefit children; it lifts the entire family. Parents feel appreciated, too, when their efforts to create a nurturing environment are celebrated.

While it's tempting to go all out with celebrations, it's important to keep things genuine. The key is to maintain a balanced perspective, ensuring that celebrations don't become overwhelming. You also don't want it to be sincere. Sometimes, the simplest gestures are the most meaningful.

A homemade card, a special dinner, or a family movie night can be just as rewarding as an extravagant outing. The focus should be on the sentiment behind the celebration rather than its scale. You're creating moments that resonate with love and appreciation. You aren't just ticking off another event on the calendar.

As you're pulling through the events of daily life, it's easy to overlook the small achievements that deserve celebration. But by taking the time to acknowledge these moments, we build an atmosphere of positivity. Celebrations become a way of life, a family tradition that reinforces the bonds that hold us together.

## 3.4 Building Trust Through Consistent Presence

Imagine you're sitting at the dinner table, and your child is recounting the day's adventures at school. Meanwhile, your phone is beeping with emails, the TV is chattering in the background, and your mind is racing through tomorrow's to-do list. Sound familiar?

Being present isn't about physical presence. It's about giving your undivided attention, both physically and emotionally, to the little humans who look up to you. Trust is built on this presence. It's the foundation of a relationship where your child feels secure.

This is what makes your child know that, despite life's whirlwind, you're there for them. This presence is the glue that holds your bond together. It's the quiet assurance that no matter what, they have a safe harbor in you.

Now, maintaining this presence amidst distractions can feel like trying to meditate in the middle of a rock concert. But with a few strategies, it becomes a bit more manageable. You can start by scheduling unplugged time with the family.

You can set aside a time each day, even if it's just 15 minutes when screens are put away, and everyone is in the moment. Maybe it's during dinner or right before bed. This dedicated time allows you to engage without the constant ping of notifications.

Practicing mindfulness during interactions also helps. Focus on the conversation at hand, noticing the tone of their voice, the sparkle in their eyes, and the stories they share. You'll all be in the moment, not just physically but with your whole heart.

**Reliability is another key ingredient** in the trust stew. It's the consistency in your actions, the follow-through on promises, and the clarity of boundaries. When you say you'll be at the soccer game or that you'll help with homework, be there. It's more than just showing up. It's about being engaged and committed.

**Setting and maintaining clear boundaries further cements reliability.** You're letting your child know what to expect from you and what you expect from them. It provides a sense of security and a stable framework within which they can explore and grow. Following through on commitments reinforces the message that they can count on you.

The impact of a strong parent-child trust relationship is great. It opens the door to enhanced communication and a level of openness that can weather the storms of growing up. When your child trusts you, they're more likely to confide in you, to share their fears and dreams.

This trust becomes a two-way street, building a relationship where both parties feel heard and respected. It's the difference between a child who shuts down after a tough day and one who seeks you out for comfort and advice.

Trust transforms the family dynamic, creating a haven where everyone feels safe to express themselves. Everyone knows they'll be met with love and understanding.

If you're dealing with distractions and demands, being present and reliable may seem like a tall order. But these efforts are a gift you give to your child and yourself. They create an environment where trust flourishes and where relationships deepen. One where your family finds its anchor amidst the chaos.

It's about making the choice to be there, fully and completely, even when life pulls you in a thousand directions. The rewards of this presence are immeasurable, enriching your family's life with connection, security, and love.

## 3.5 Empathy Exercises for Family Unity

Empathy is the secret ingredient that transforms a house into a home. It goes beyond understanding alone. It's feeling along with someone else. In families, empathy creates a climate of compassion and connection. It allows each member to feel valued and heard.

When empathy is the foundation, interactions become more compassionate, and conflicts are resolved with love rather than grumbles. You're putting yourself in someone else's shoes, not just seeing the world through their eyes. Instead, you're genuinely feeling their emotions.

This understanding creates harmony, a gentle rhythm where everyone feels like they belong. Building empathy within the family isn't just for the kids; it's a family affair. **Role-playing different family scenarios can be a fun** and insightful way to develop empathy.

Picture this: one child plays the parent, the other a sibling, and they switch roles to understand each other's perspectives. It'll be like a mini theater session without the need for costumes. Through role-playing, family members can express how they feel in various situations, helping others understand their viewpoints.

**Another approach is sharing daily gratitude practices**. Each family member takes turns expressing gratitude for something that happened during their day. This practice shifts focus from the negatives and builds an appreciation for each other's experiences, enabling empathy and understanding.

Empathy-driven families enjoy a supportive home environment. When empathy is part of daily life, conflicts shrink, and cooperation blooms. There's a noticeable reduction in misunderstandings, as each person takes a moment to consider the emotions behind others' actions.

This doesn't mean disagreements vanish, but they're approached with a mindset focused on resolution rather than confrontation. An empathetic family is like a team that listens, supports, and collaborates. All these lead to a more peaceful and cooperative household.

It's a domino effect; one empathetic interaction inspires another, creating a culture of kindness and respect. Incorporating empathy into everyday life doesn't require grand gestures. You can begin with simple, active empathy check-ins.

These are brief moments where you genuinely ask each family member how they're feeling and listen without interruption. You can use this time to acknowledge their emotions, whether it's excitement over a new hobby or disappointment from a bad day at school. Encouraging empathetic discussions during family meetings also helps.

These meetings can include sharing feelings about recent events and brainstorming ways to support each other. You'll be creating a safe space where everyone feels comfortable expressing themselves, knowing they'll be met with understanding.

Remember that empathy is about creating a home where everyone feels seen and understood. A home where love is expressed through actions and words. When empathy is inculcated in daily life, it strengthens the bonds that hold the family together.

Each act of empathy is a step towards unity, a reminder that despite the chaos of life, we have each other. With empathy as our guide, we move forward in our quest for a home filled with harmony and love.

Now, let's take this compassionate spirit and explore the next chapter. This is a chapter where we'll walk through effective time management techniques that support our family's growth.

# Chapter 4

## *Your Dedication to Reflection and Refinement*

Imagine your family as a bunch of musicians in a band. Everyone has their instrument and their part to play, but if you're not tuned into each other, It can sound more like a clattering mess than a harmonious symphony. That's where family feedback sessions come into play.

These are more than meetings. They're your band practice, where everyone gets to tune their instruments and find their rhythm together. Creating a safe space for this kind of honest dialogue is essential.

It's like giving everyone a backstage pass to express their needs and concerns. And, believe me, this can transform your family's situation.

So **how do you kick off these feedback sessions without them feeling like a corporate board meeting?** First, you need to set a consistent time and place. Think of it as your regular gig slot. Maybe it's Sunday afternoons with snacks in hand, or perhaps Tuesday nights after dinner, when everyone can unwind and chat.

When you establish this routine, you help everyone know when and where to be. This sets the stage for open and productive conversations. To keep things orderly and ensure everyone gets a turn, consider using a talking stick or another object. It might sound a bit campfire-and-s'mores, but it works.

It's a simple way to indicate whose turn it is to speak. You want to make sure no one dominates the discussion, so that everyone can feel heard.

**Participation is key**, and getting everyone to chime in can sometimes feel like pulling teeth. But fear not. There are ways to encourage even the youngest members to share their thoughts. Kids, especially, might need a little nudge.

Try creating an atmosphere where they feel comfortable speaking up. You can use prompts or questions to stimulate discussion. Ask open-ended questions like:

*"What was something that made you happy this week?"*

Or

*"If you could change one thing about our family routine, what would it be?"*

These questions can spark conversation and make everyone feel that their voice matters.

The magic of feedback lies in its ability to foster growth. It's not just about talking; it's about listening, learning, and acting on what's shared. Documenting feedback outcomes and action plans can be a game-changer.

Keep a simple notebook or a digital document where you jot down the key points and agreed-upon actions. This record helps you track progress and shows your commitment to improvement. It's like having a set list of your family's goals and plans, helping everyone stay accountable and focused.

By acting on feedback, you demonstrate that these sessions are more than just talk. You'll be showing that they're a commitment to making changes that benefit everyone.

## 4.1 The Family Feedback Journal

You should consider starting a Family Feedback Journal. You can use it to document each session's highlights and action items. Try encouraging everyone to contribute, even the kids.

The journal is not just a record – it's a living document that reflects your family's journey. Also, check back on past entries to see how far you've come and celebrate the wins along the way.

Regular feedback sessions can transform your family's interactions, turning potential discord into harmony. They're an opportunity for everyone to connect, share, and grow together.

By dedicating time to these conversations, you create a culture of openness and mutual respect. You want to tune in to each other and fine-tune those family dynamics. What you seek to achieve is for your collective melody to shine through beautifully.

## 4.2 Assessing Success: What Worked, What Didn't

We all know that life with kids can be unpredictable and sometimes downright chaotic. That's why regular assessments of your routines and strategies are like a secret weapon for creating positive change.

By taking a step back and evaluating what's working and where things are going off the rails, you can make adjustments. These adjustments can lead to smoother days and happier families. You want to identify patterns of success and areas of struggle.

Maybe you've noticed that bedtime is a nightly battle, but

breakfast is a breeze. Or perhaps you realize that the kids are thriving with their new chore chart, but family game night is more of a flop. These insights are gold. They help you focus your energy on what's working while tackling the areas that need a little more attention.

To get started, consider using tools like a family success journal. This is a place where you can jot down your observations, victories, and challenges. It's like a diary for your parenting highs and lows. It gives you a space to reflect on what's going well and what's causing those hair-pulling moments.

Another idea is to create a "*success and setbacks*" board. This visual tool allows everyone in the family to contribute by noting achievements and obstacles.

It's like a family scoreboard, and seeing your progress (or lack thereof) in black and white can be incredibly motivating. Plus, it creates a sense of teamwork as everyone works together to improve.

Learning from setbacks is where the real growth happens. It's easy to get discouraged when things don't go as planned. However, understanding failures can lead to better strategies and resilience.

When something doesn't work out, analyze it without assigning blame.

*Was the goal realistic?*

*Were there external factors at play?*

*Could a different approach yield better results?*

By examining setbacks with curiosity, you can uncover valuable lessons and develop strategies that are more effective. This approach teaches kids that it's okay to make mistakes as long as they learn and grow from them.

Maintaining an objective perspective is crucial during these assessments. It's easy to fall into the trap of self-criticism or frustration when things don't go as planned. Instead, encourage a mindset of curiosity and openness.

Approach each assessment with the attitude of a scientist observing an experiment.

*What variables are at play?*

*What patterns are emerging?*

This detachment allows you to see things clearly and make adjustments without the emotional baggage. You're seeking to practice observation and using what you learn to make informed decisions.

Incorporating regular assessments into your routine doesn't have to be a chore. It can be as simple as taking a few minutes each week to reflect on what's working and what isn't. It's a time to celebrate your successes, big and small. It's a time to strategize how to tackle those persistent challenges.

Making assessments a regular part of your family routine helps you create a culture of continuous improvement and growth. You're nurturing a family environment that's adaptable and resilient. A family that's always striving to be a little better each day.

Through these assessments, you'll find that what once seemed like insurmountable obstacles become opportunities for growth.

## 4.3 Iterating and Realigning Family Goals

Setting family goals is like planning a road trip with kids. You start with a destination in mind, but sometimes, you need to take detours or make unexpected stops along the way. That's where the magic of iteration comes in.

Iteration in goal setting means regularly revisiting and refining your goals to ensure they remain relevant and achievable. It's like checking your GPS every so often to make sure you're still on the right track. Even if you've taken a few scenic routes or pit stops.

**This process involves regular reviews and updates**, where you gather the family around the metaphorical map. You all sit to discuss what's working and what needs tweaking.

Maybe the original goal of having weekly game nights needs to shift to biweekly because of everyone's busy schedules. That's okay. Realigning keeps goals fresh and attainable.

Now, let's talk about aligning these goals with your family's continuously changing values and priorities. You're ensuring your goals are wearing the right outfit for the occasion. As your family grows and circumstances change, what you value might shift too.

Maybe when you first set a goal to save for a big vacation, your focus was on adventure. Now, with the kids getting older, perhaps education and learning experiences take precedence. Involving the whole family in this realignment process is crucial.

It's a team huddle where everyone gets a say. Ask each family member what they think should be prioritized and why. This ensures that goals reflect current circumstances and also promotes a sense of investment from everyone involved.

Flexibility in goal-setting doesn't just lead to greater success; it brings satisfaction too. When you remain adaptable, you open the door to celebrating small victories along the way. These mini-celebrations are like the rest stops on your road trip. They're necessary breaks that keep spirits high and motivation strong.

Maybe you've had to adjust the timeline for a goal. Perhaps you've achieved something smaller en route to a larger objective. Don't let these moments pass uncelebrated. They're milestones that reflect progress and perseverance. They remind everyone that you're moving forward, even if the pace isn't always as fast as you'd like.

Let's look at **real-life examples of families who've successfully iterated their goals.**

Take ***the Williams family***, for instance. They initially set a goal to eat dinner together every night. But with Dad's new job requiring late hours, this became nearly impossible. Instead of scrapping the goal, they adapted it.

Now, they do family breakfasts instead. Savoring scrambled eggs and sharing stories before the day begins.

Or consider ***the Smith family***, who aimed for a monthly family outing. They found that conflicting schedules made this difficult. So they shifted to quarterly weekend trips instead, allowing for more planning and anticipation.

These stories show that flexibility and iteration aren't just about adjusting. It's about finding what works and making it meaningful.

In essence, iterating and realigning family goals is about maintaining momentum while embracing the twists and turns of life. You're recognizing that while the destination may remain the same, the path to getting there can change, and that's perfectly okay.

This approach ensures that goals remain relevant and also strengthens family bonds as everyone works together. You all adapt and celebrate each step along the way.

## 4.4 Creating a Family Vision Board

Imagine a giant canvas, blank and full of potential, waiting to be filled with your family's dreams and aspirations. That's the essence of a family vision board. A vibrant collage of goals that brings clarity and motivation to everyone involved.

Visualization is a powerful tool because it turns abstract wishes into something tangible and visible. It's like having a north star guiding your family's decisions and actions. When you see your goals every day, they become more than just thoughts in your head. They begin to transform into a shared mission.

**There's a connection between visualization and success** and it's well-documented. People who regularly visualize their goals are more likely to achieve them. This is so, because they keep their aspirations at the forefront of their minds.

Creating a vision board is more than cutting and pasting pictures onto a board. It's a thoughtful process that starts with a family brainstorming session. Gather around and discuss what each member of the family hopes to achieve in the coming months or years.

Once you have your ideas, choose a central location for the

board. It can be somewhere everyone passes by daily. This constant exposure serves as a gentle reminder of your shared goals.

Next, gather a mix of images, words, and quotes that resonate with each family member's aspirations. Magazines, online printouts, and even personal photos can all contribute to the board's unique tapestry.

The beauty of a vision board lies in its ability to maintain focus and alignment. It's not a static piece of art; it's a living document that should evolve with your family's goals. You can make it a habit to update and review the board regularly.

Monthly check-ins can be an excellent opportunity to assess progress, celebrate accomplishments, and adjust any goals that need tweaking. These sessions are like recalibrating your compass, ensuring that everyone is still heading in the right direction. Keeping the board current can help you maintain its relevance as you continue to inspire action.

Note that getting the whole family involved in the creation of the vision board can turn it into a memorable project. Try hosting a vision board creation day where everyone gathers with scissors, glue, and a plethora of art supplies. You can think of it as a crafting party, complete with snacks and music.

Encourage each person to contribute their ideas and creativity. This makes the board a true reflection of the family's collective dreams. Using collaborative art supplies like markers, stickers, and colored paper can make the process even more fun.

When you engage in shared activities like this, you strengthen family bonds. You also ensure that everyone has a stake in the board's meaning and goals.

A family vision board is more than a decorative piece. It's a dynamic tool that encourages growth, unity, and motivation. While working together to build and maintain your board, you're creating a visual representation of your family's values and aspirations.

It serves as a daily reminder of what you're working towards, aiding a sense of collaboration. Whenever you all get lost in busy schedules, the vision board stands as a beacon of inspiration. It guides your family through challenges and celebrates the victories along the way.

### 4.5 Celebrating Growth and Adaptability

Imagine the delight on a child's face when you acknowledge their effort in learning to tie their shoelaces. Or the pride they feel when you notice their determination in improving their reading skills. Recognizing growth is more than the outcome. **It's encouraging the journey of development and resilience**.

Celebrating these achievements, however small, sends a powerful message. It shows that **effort is valued and growth is celebrated**. It's like planting seeds of motivation that flourish into a lifelong love for learning and personal development.

When children feel their progress is noticed, they're more likely to continue striving towards their goals. This is emboldened by the acknowledgment of their hard work.

Celebrating family achievements doesn't have to be an extravagant affair. Sometimes, the simplest gestures are the most meaningful. Consider creating a "*growth wall*" in a prominent place in your home.

This could be a section of the wall where you display achievements, both big and small. Use sticky notes, photos, or drawings to showcase progress. It's a breathing encouragement of the family's dedication and adaptability.

Another idea is to *host a family appreciation day.* It doesn't need to be a big event. It can be a special day where everyone's achievements are recognized and celebrated.

You might prepare favorite meals, share stories of accomplishments, and take turns expressing gratitude for each other's efforts. These celebrations reinforce the importance of growth and adaptability. It makes everyone feel valued and appreciated.

Adaptability plays a significant role in family success. It's the ability to adjust to new circumstances and find creative solutions to challenges. Sharing stories of adaptability within the family can be a powerful way to inspire this trait.

Perhaps there was a time when a family vacation didn't go as planned, but everyone pitched in to make it memorable regardless. Or maybe a project at work required late nights, and the family rallied to support each other in managing household tasks.

These stories highlight the strength of flexibility and the importance of working together to overcome obstacles. They serve as reminders that while plans may change, family love and support remain constant.

Gratitude for growth is like the glue that holds all these elements together. Practicing gratitude helps us recognize and appreciate the progress we make, both individually and collectively. Consider incorporating daily gratitude journaling into your family routine. It doesn't have to be a lengthy exercise. A simple note about something you're grateful for can suffice.

Encourage each family member to reflect on their personal growth and the growth they've witnessed in others. This practice breeds a positive mindset and reinforces the importance of appreciating the journey, not just the destination.

Focusing on gratitude helps you create an environment where growth is celebrated. An environment where adaptability is embraced, ensuring a supportive and nurturing family dynamic.

As we bring this chapter to a close, the essence of growth and adaptability in family life becomes clear. It's recognizing the small steps that lead to significant change and celebrating the progress that often goes unnoticed.

It is enabling an environment where everyone feels valued and supported. Through creative celebrations, shared stories, and a focus on gratitude, families can cultivate resilience. They can inculcate adaptability, setting the stage for continued success and satisfaction.

In the next chapter, we'll explore how these principles can be applied to managing time effectively. That way ensures that family life remains balanced, fulfilling, and joyously chaotic in the best possible way.

# Chapter 5

## *Effective Time Management Techniques*

Picture this: it's dawn, and the house is eerily quiet. You tiptoe out of bed, savoring the rare tranquility before the storm of activity that is your morning routine. But, oh, the magic of those few, precious minutes when you are alone with your thoughts and a steaming cup of coffee!

It's the calm before the kids wake up, and the rush ensues. This is the secret of an organized morning—one that sets a positive, serene tone for the day ahead. A smooth start can transform the entire family's mood, helping everyone face the day with a smile instead of a scowl.

Simplifying morning chaos begins with preparation. It's building a routine that doesn't feel like a military operation but still gets everyone out the door on time, sanity intact. You can begin the night before by preparing outfits and packing lunches.

Imagine waking up to find everything ready, like a mini gift from past you to future you. It saves precious minutes and prevents those frantic searches for matching socks or favorite superhero shirts.

Consistency is key, so aim for a set wake-up time. It might seem impossible at first, but once you adjust, it becomes a natural part of your rhythm. Your body and mind will thank you for the predictability.

**Distractions can derail even the best-laid morning plans**. That's why minimizing them is essential. Consider creating a no-screen rule during breakfast. I know I know—screens are the ultimate morning babysitter. But hear me out. Without the distraction of phones or tablets, breakfast can become a time for family connection.

You might find your kids actually talking to you, sharing dreams they had, or simply recounting the latest playground drama. It's a chance for everyone to engage, listen, and start the day with a sense of togetherness.

A calm morning routine doesn't just mean less stress; it can also lead to better moods and increased productivity throughout the day. Think of it as the first domino in a chain reaction. When mornings run smoothly, the rest of the day often follows suit.

Kids head off to school feeling centered, which can improve their focus and behavior. You head to work with a clearer mind, ready to tackle whatever challenges come your way. Enhanced family communication over breakfast strengthens bonds and sets a positive tone. One that resonates well beyond the morning hours.

## 5.1 The Morning Routine Checklist

You might want to consider creating a morning routine checklist to guide your family through each step. List tasks like

*"Get dressed,"*

*"Eat breakfast,"*

*"Pack backpack."*

And more...

Hang it where everyone can see, using stickers or check marks to track completion. This promotes independence and also turns the routine into a collaborative family effort.

Mastering the morning can feel like conquering *Everest* when schedules are tight. But with a bit of planning, a sprinkle of consistency, and minimizing distractions, you can transform the start of your day.

It's about reclaiming those precious morning moments, turning them from chaotic to calm. By doing this, you'll set a positive tone for everyone as they head out into the world.

## 5.2 Streamlining Meal Preparation

Let's say you come home after a long, exhausting day at work, only to face the dreaded question: "*What's for dinner?*" If you're like most busy parents, this scenario is all too familiar. But fear not, because efficient meal prep is here to save the day.

It's about saving time and reducing the stress that comes with the daily dinner scramble. When you've got meals ready to go, it's like you've got a magic wand that keeps you in a state of calm.

Plus, when you plan, you're less likely to succumb to the

temptations of takeout. Won't that be a win for both your wallet and your waistline? With a bit of planning, you can nourish your family with healthier choices without sacrificing your sanity.

Meal prep starts with a solid plan. Trying to create a weekly meal calendar is your first step. Picture this: a simple chart with slots for each day's dinner, maybe even lunch and breakfast too. That's if you're feeling ambitious. Once you have a plan, stick it on your fridge for easy reference.

There, you've gotten your own personal assistant that reminds you of what's on the menu. Also, batch cooking is another game-changer. You can spend a couple of hours on the weekend whipping up big batches of staples like rice, quinoa, or roasted veggies, and stash them in the fridge.

This way, you can mix and match these building blocks throughout the week, creating new dishes with minimal effort. And let's not forget about the wonders of your freezer. Cook once, eat twice, or even thrice! You can double your recipes and freeze half for those days when cooking feels uneasy.

Getting the family involved in meal prep can turn a chore into a bonding experience. Assign age-appropriate tasks to the kids. Even toddlers can get in on the action. Give them simple jobs like washing lettuce or stirring a pot. Older kids can tackle more complex tasks like chopping vegetables or measuring ingredients.

It's a great way to teach them valuable life skills while easing some of your workload. Plus, kids are more likely to eat what they've helped prepare. And, that's a blessing if you're dealing with picky eaters. This collaborative effort makes meal prep less of a solo slog and more of a family affair. You'll have everyone pitching in to create delicious meals.

Now, let's talk about quick and healthy meals because no one has time to spend hours in the kitchen every night. **Simple one-pot or sheet-pan dinners are lifesavers**. Imagine tossing some chicken, potatoes, and broccoli onto a sheet pan. You drizzle with olive oil and seasonings and let the oven do the work. Dinner practically makes itself!

**Slow cookers and Instant Pots are another secret weapon**. They can turn a jumble of ingredients into a savory masterpiece with minimal effort. You can throw in some beans, diced tomatoes, and spices in the morning. And, by dinnertime, you've got a hearty chili that's sure to please even the pickiest of palates.

Embracing meal prep is more than saving time or reducing stress. You're creating a rhythm that supports your family's well-being. The benefits ripple out, affecting not just your evenings but your whole week. You find yourself with more time to relax, connect, and enjoy the company of your family. All the while knowing that you're feeding them nutritious, home-cooked meals.

With a bit of planning, a dash of teamwork, and creativity, meal prep can become a cherished part of your weekly routine. One that nourishes both body and soul.

## 5.3 Visual Schedules: A Parent's Best Friend

Imagine walking into a room and immediately spotting a colorful chart that lays out your entire day. Instantly, your mind feels at ease. That's the magic of visual schedules, a tool that turns everything around beautifully. This happens when family tasks are organized with precision.

Visual schedules aren't just for kids; they're a lifesaver for the entire family. They act as a visual reminder of what needs to be done, reducing anxiety by providing a clear roadmap for the day.

It's like having a personal assistant who keeps everyone on track, making the overwhelming manageable. When everyone knows what's coming next, mornings become smoother. In the same way, afternoons become less frazzled and evenings more relaxed.

Creating an effective visual schedule doesn't require a degree in graphic design. You can start with a simple chart and get creative. Use color-coded sections for each family member. For example, you can use blue for Dad, pink for Mom, and green for the kids.

This way, everyone knows which tasks belong to them at a glance. Incorporate visual cues like images or icons. Little ones who can't read yet will appreciate a picture of a toothbrush for brushing time or a backpack for school prep.

These visual aids in making the schedule more engaging and also help non-readers understand their tasks. You can hang this masterpiece in a central location, like the kitchen or hallway, where everyone can see it. That way, It becomes a communal hub, a place where the family gathers to check in on the day's events.

Visual schedules are more than just organizational tools; they're powerful for building independence in children. When kids see their tasks laid out, they're empowered to take charge of their routines. It's a bit like giving them the keys to their own little world.

They learn to manage their time, completing activities without constant reminders. This sense of responsibility boosts their confidence and teaches valuable time-management skills, which will serve them well beyond childhood. So, instead of nagging, you might find yourself quietly cheering them on as they tick off each task.

Customization is where the fun really begins. **Personalizing schedules to fit your family's unique needs can turn a functional tool into a fun art project**. Use family photos or themes that resonate with everyone.

Perhaps your family loves superheroes. Why not create a schedule where each task is a mission to be completed? Or maybe you all share a love for animals. You can assign each task to a different animal guide.

The possibilities are endless, and the more personalized the schedule, the more engaged everyone will be. It becomes a reflection of your family's personality, a piece of art that not only organizes but also inspires.

Visual schedules can transform the way your family operates. They provide clarity and structure, reduce stress, and build independence. They're a simple yet effective way to ensure everyone knows what's happening and when.

You'll be turning a potentially chaotic day into a series of well-coordinated events. While embracing the power of visual scheduling, you might just find that your home runs a little smoother. You might see that your kids are a little more self-reliant and your days are filled with a bit of peace.

## 5.4 The Art of Delegation in Family Tasks

Assuming it's the end of a long day, and you're staring at a mountain of laundry, a sink full of dishes, and a to-do list that seems to have its own to-do list. Sound familiar? It's the classic tale of the overstretched parent.

But what if I told you there's a secret sauce to managing this heartache? It's called delegation, and it's about time we use it. Sharing responsibilities isn't just about lightening your load. It's about enabling teamwork within the family.

When everyone chips in, it creates a sense of unity and purpose. This reduces stress and makes life a little more manageable. Plus, it teaches valuable life skills to the kids, like:

- Responsibility
- Time management
- The importance of contributing to a team effort. And more…

When you think about delegation, start by matching tasks to family members' strengths. Maybe your partner has a knack for organization, which would be perfect for tackling the grocery list and pantry organization. Your oldest might be a budding chef eager to help with dinner prep.

Even the youngest can have their role, like setting the table or sorting laundry by color. Assigning tasks based on skill and interest helps you get the job done. You'll also be engaging everyone in a way that feels natural and rewarding.

Rotating chores can keep things fair and engaging. That way, you'll prevent boredom and ensure that no one feels stuck with the less glamorous tasks. It's like a game of musical chairs but with chores—one that keeps everyone on their toes!

Now, let's talk about **cooperation and accountability**, which can sometimes feel like a herculean task. You can set clear expectations and timelines for each task. Clarity is your friend here. When everyone knows exactly what's expected and by when, it's easier to stay on track.

Consider using a family task board to track progress. It's a visual reminder of what needs to be done and by whom. Plus, there's something oddly satisfying about ticking off a completed task. It's like a mini celebration every time!

Encourage kids to update the board themselves. It instills a sense of ownership. After all, it's all about creating a system where everyone is accountable yet supported.

Delegation isn't just about getting chores done; it's about strengthening the family bond. Shared responsibilities build trust and mutual respect. When everyone pulls their weight, it enables appreciation for what each person contributes.

It's like assembling a puzzle, where each piece is crucial to the bigger picture. These shared tasks open up opportunities for communication and collaboration, turning mundane chores into moments of connection. You find yourselves chatting over dishes or laughing while folding laundry. Suddenly, these tasks become less of a burden and more of a shared experience.

As life swings you in different directions, delegation is a thread that weaves everything together. It lightens the load, teaches valuable skills, and strengthens the bonds that hold us together. It's about recognizing that we're all in this together, each playing an essential role in the family machine.

So, as you stand before that mountain of chores, remember that you don't have to climb it alone. You've got a team ready and willing to tackle it together. And, who knows, you might just find that with a bit of delegation, those chores turn into cherished family memories.

## 5.5 Balancing Work and Family Life Seamlessly

Balancing work and family life can often feel like walking a tightrope while juggling flaming torches. The pressures of managing dual roles can leave you feeling stretched thin. Much like butter over too much bread. It's a common struggle for many parents who are trying to keep up with career commitments while ensuring their family doesn't feel like an afterthought.

The impact of work-life imbalance can be profound. It affects not just your well-being but also the emotional climate of your home. When work spills into family time, it can lead to feelings of guilt and stress. There's also the nagging worry that you're not doing enough on either front.

**Practical strategies for achieving balance can be a lifesaver**. You can start by establishing clear boundaries between work and home time. Think of it as drawing a line in the sand. Like a protective barrier that ensures work doesn't encroach on family moments.

This might mean turning off email notifications after hours or designating a specific workspace if you're working from home. The key is to create mental and physical separation between your professional and personal life.

Technology can also be your ally, offering flexibility that was unimaginable a decade ago. Tools like shared calendars or communication apps can help manage schedules. That way, you'll be ensuring both work and family commitments are met without one overshadowing the other.

Prioritizing family time is crucial in this balancing act. Intentional scheduling can make a world of difference. It can transform family interactions from fleeting moments to cherished traditions.

Consider creating dedicated family nights or activities, like a weekly game night or a Sunday afternoon hike. These scheduled times become sacred. It becomes an opportunity for everyone to unplug from their individual pursuits and connect as a unit.

When family time is prioritized, it sends a message to your loved ones that they are valued and important. It strengthens relationships and creates a sense of security. It also provides a buffer against the stresses of the outside world.

Amidst the chaos, maintaining personal well-being is often the first thing to slip through the cracks. Yet, taking time for yourself is not a luxury; it's a necessity. Practicing self-care rituals can be as simple as:

- A nightly bubble bath.

- Morning yoga session.
- A quiet cup of coffee before the house wakes, among others.

These moments are your lifeline, allowing you to recharge and face the day with renewed energy. Scheduling regular downtime for relaxation is equally important. Block out time in your calendar – just as you would for a work meeting. Do this to simply exist without an agenda. It's a moment to breathe, reflect, and recalibrate.

While pulling through the complexities of work and family life, remember that it's not about achieving perfect balance every day. Some days work will demand more of you; other days, family will take center stage.

The goal is to find a rhythm that works for you, one that allows you to fulfill your responsibilities while nurturing the relationships that matter most. So, embrace the imperfections and be kind to yourself. You're doing the best you can, and that's enough.

In this chapter, we've explored practical ways to balance the demands of work and family life, from setting boundaries to prioritizing time together. As you move forward, keep in mind that balance is an ongoing practice, not a one-time achievement.

The strategies discussed are stepping stones to a more harmonious life—one where both work and family thrive. In the next chapter, we'll discuss positive discipline strategies for active kids and help you create a loving, respectful environment at home.

# Chapter 6

## *Positive Discipline for Active Kids*

Sometimes, it could be a sunny Saturday morning, and you're looking forward to a peaceful breakfast with the family. Then, out of nowhere, your kid decides the living room couch is actually a trampoline. Before you know it, there's chaos. Is this familiar?

This chapter is all about understanding those moments when our little ones seem to transform into little storms. They can leave a trail of mayhem in their wake. But don't worry. There's a reason behind those outbursts. Understanding it is the key to turning chaos into calm.

### 6.1 Understanding Child Behavior Triggers

Let's talk about behavior triggers. These are the little things that can flip your child's switch from angel to, well, not-so-angelic. When you recognize these triggers, it's like you've got a secret map of your child's emotional landscape. Common triggers include:

- Hunger
- Fatigue
- Overstimulation, etc.

Do you remember that time when you were hangry and snapped at your partner for no reason? Kids feel that, too, but with less control. Environmental factors play a huge role as well. A crowded, noisy room can be overwhelming for a child.

It's like trying to work in a bustling café with a marching band playing next door. When you understand these triggers, it helps you through those tricky moments with foresight. You'll also be empathetic towards the child.

Tracking these triggers might sound like a chore, but it's actually quite enlightening. Consider keeping a behavior journal. You can jot down incidents when your child's behavior takes a nosedive. Also note the time, setting, and any potential triggers.

Over time, patterns will emerge, helping you pinpoint what sets off those meltdowns. Observing changes in behavior can also be a game-changer.

Maybe your kid's more likely to throw a fit after a long day at daycare or when they're hungry. Identifying these patterns allows you to take proactive measures. You can ensure that they have a snack after school or scheduling quiet time after a busy day.

Once you understand these triggers, you're in a position to tailor your discipline strategies to your child's needs. Instead of reacting in the heat of the moment, you can plan ahead.

For instance, if you know your child tends to get cranky when they're tired, adjust their schedule to include more time for rest. If overstimulation is a trigger, create a calm-down corner in your home where they can retreat when things get too hectic.

When you address the root cause, you'll stop managing behavior only. You'll be helping your child learn to regulate their emotions.

Preventing these triggers is the ultimate goal. You'll find that establishing consistent routines can work wonders. Kids thrive on predictability. It's like giving them a roadmap to their day. So, knowing what comes next can ease anxiety and reduce the likelihood of outbursts.

Also, creating a calm and predictable environment is equally important. Try to keep your home a sanctuary and not a circus. You'll be amazed at the difference that soft lighting, minimal clutter, and designated play areas can make.

### The Behavior Trigger Tracker

You might want to try creating a behavior trigger tracker. It could be a simple chart where you record incidents, potential triggers, and the environment. With time, this will help you identify patterns and adjust your strategies for a more peaceful home.

When you grasp these behavior triggers and address them, you'll be eliminating a lot of challenges. You'll be equipping both you and your child with the tools to handle these challenges easily. It's about turning those couch-jumping mornings into opportunities for connection.

## 6.2 Setting Boundaries with Love and Logic

Let's imagine for a moment that boundaries are the invisible fences that keep a child's world safe. Kids, despite their protests, actually crave these boundaries because they provide a sense of security. Without them, they might feel like you're asking them to navigate a maze without walls, and they don't know which way to turn or what's expected of them.

You see, clear boundaries help children develop self-discipline and an understanding of limits. They are necessary for their emotional and social development.

They learn what behaviors are acceptable and which aren't. These pave the way for healthy decision-making as they grow. And trust me, when kids know the rules of the game, they're much less likely to test them.

Now, let's talk about setting these boundaries with what I like to call a "love and logic" approach. This method combines empathy with firm rules, creating a balance that respects both the child's feelings and the family's needs. It's about guiding children with kindness while maintaining clear expectations.

Imagine it as the difference between a drill sergeant barking orders and a wise mentor offering guidance. Respectful and firm communication is key. It's about using a tone that conveys authority without aggression.

You'll be ensuring your child knows you mean business but that you're also on their side. It's the kind of communication that says, "I understand that you're upset about bedtime, but staying up late isn't an option."

So, **how do you set these boundaries effectively?** Well, you can start with simple language. Kids need clarity, not cryptic riddles about what they can and cannot do. Explain the rules in straightforward terms they can grasp.

Instead of saying, "*You should know better than to leave your toys everywhere,*" try, "*Toys belong in the toy box when you're done playing.*"

Consistency is another essential piece of the puzzle. If bedtime is 8 pm today, it shouldn't be 9 pm tomorrow just because you're feeling generous. Consistency helps reinforce the boundaries you're setting.

You'll be making it easier for your child to understand and adhere to them. It's like a steady drumbeat in the background of their lives, providing a rhythm they can count on.

Now, let's explore the role of natural consequences in boundary setting. Allowing children to experience the consequences of their actions is a powerful teaching tool. It's about letting the world teach sometimes.

For instance, if your child refuses to wear a coat on a chilly day, they'll likely feel cold and learn why coats are important. Of course, discretion is used to ensure safety, but when appropriate, natural consequences teach responsibility.

Also, decision-making is far more effective than lectures ever could. It's about balancing guidance with autonomy. You want to give your child the space to make mistakes and learn from them without feeling abandoned.

Everyday situations offer ample opportunities to apply this approach. If your child forgets their homework, have them face the teacher's response rather than swooping in to save the day. If they choose to spend all their allowance on candy, let them experience running out of money before the next allowance day.

These experiences teach invaluable lessons about responsibility and the real-world implications of their choices. You want to help them understand that while you're there to guide them, the quality of their decisions directly impacts the quality of their lives.

As you pass through this balance between love and logic, remember that boundaries are not just about saying "*no*." They're about creating a framework within which your child can safely explore the world. One where they can develop autonomy and learn the skills they need to thrive. It's about showing them that while you have high expectations, your love and support are unwavering.

### 6.3 Redirecting Energy Through Structured Play

Let's say your little one is bouncing off the walls like a pinball, and you're just trying to keep your sanity intact. High-energy kids often seem like they've got a motor that never stops. But channeling that boundless energy into structured play can work wonders.

It's not just about burning off steam. It's about giving them the tools to manage their own energy levels. Structured play has a lot of benefits:

- **Physically**, it helps kids develop strength, coordination, and motor skills.
- **Emotionally**, it provides an outlet for them to express themselves and work through feelings in a safe environment.
- **Socially**, play teaches cooperation, turn-taking, and communication.

It's like a triple whammy of goodness, all wrapped up in a fun package.

Let's talk about activities. Think of structured play as organized chaos. A little bit of order amidst the natural whirlwind of childhood energy. **Obstacle courses** are fantastic for this. You can set up a simple course in your backyard or living room using cushions, chairs, and toys.

Kids love the challenge, and it gives them a sense of accomplishment as they complete it. Or try a **scavenger hunt**. You can create a list of items for them to find around the house or yard. It's a great way to direct their focus and curiosity.

**Team sports or cooperative games** are perfect, too. They not only promote physical health but also teach kids how to work together towards a common goal. They'll learn the value of teamwork while having a blast.

Balancing structure and freedom is key. Kids need the security of a framework while also having the freedom to explore and create. It's like giving them a blank canvas with just enough guidelines to keep them on track.

You can set up play zones with open-ended materials like blocks, art supplies, or dress-up clothes. These areas provide a structured environment but allow for endless creativity. Try rotating play activities to keep things fresh and exciting.

You can have one week of building with LEGO, and the next could be focused on art projects. This keeps your child engaged and prevents boredom from setting in.

Even with busy schedules, incorporating play into daily routines is doable. Consider scheduling regular playtime sessions. It could be as simple as setting aside 30 minutes after school for structured activities. Treat it like an appointment that can't be missed. Or, find ways to blend play into chores or daily tasks.

Turn cleaning up toys into a race or make sorting laundry a color-matching game. These little tweaks turn some chores into opportunities for learning and fun. You'll be making chores less of a battle and more of a cooperative effort.

Structured play is more than just an outlet for excess energy. It's a foundation for growth. So, engaging in these activities helps children learn to channel their energy positively. They learn to build essential skills and develop a sense of discipline – all while having a great time.

It's about finding that sweet spot where they can be themselves, express their creativity, and still have enough structure to feel secure. So, while you might sometimes feel like you're living in a circus, remember that each task or game is a step towards helping your child become happy.

Know that you're making them balanced individuals. And who knows, you might even find yourself having a bit of fun along the way.

### 6.4 Non-Confrontational Language for Boundaries

Assuming you're at the playground, and your kiddo's about to attempt a daring leap off the slide. Your instinct might be to shout, "*Don't you dare!*" But what if there was a way to steer them away from risky behavior without the drama?

Let's walk you through non-confrontational communication. One where the words you choose can turn potential power struggles into cooperative exchanges. Language isn't just about getting kids to do what you want. It's about enabling an environment where they feel respected and heard.

So, choosing positive words can transform a tense situation into a teachable moment. This approach encourages cooperation and reduces resistance. You'll be making it easier for kids to follow the rules and understand expectations.

Instead of barking orders, try switching up your phrasing. For example, replace "*You must clean your room now!*" with "*I need you to tidy up your room before dinner.*"

This subtle shift in language takes the edge off. You'll be making it feel less like a command and more like a collaborative request. Offering choices is another powerful tool. Instead of saying, "*Stop playing and get ready for bed,*" try, "*Would you like to brush your teeth first or put on your pajamas?*"

Giving kids a sense of control over their actions can make them more willing to cooperate. These small changes in language can make a big difference in how children respond. You'll be reducing defiance and encouraging them to take responsibility for their actions.

But words aren't the only thing that matters. How you say them is equally important. Imagine trying to calm a storm with a hurricane. If your tone is harsh or your body language is closed off, even the most thoughtfully chosen words can fall flat. Maintaining a calm and steady tone helps keep the peace, especially during tense situations.

Your voice can be a soothing balm that de-escalated potential conflicts. Pair this with open and inviting body language. Kneel down to your child's level, make eye contact, and use gentle gestures. These non-verbal cues communicate that you're approachable and ready to listen. It creates a safe space for dialogue.

This style of communication isn't just about getting through the day without tears or tantrums. It's about building trust and understanding in your relationship with your child. When you approach them with respect and empathy, they learn to do the same.

This enables a sense of mutual respect, creating a foundation for open communication that can carry through to their teenage years and beyond. With time, your child will see you as a partner in their growth rather than an adversary to be challenged.

You'll be building a bridge of trust, where they feel safe to express themselves and seek guidance without fear of judgment.

The impact of non-confrontational language extends beyond the immediate moment. It sets the tone for how communication happens within the family. It's about creating an environment where voices are heard, and feelings are respected. It makes everyone feel valued.

When children experience communication that respects their autonomy, they're more likely to mirror that behavior. This won't be happening at home alone, but in their interactions with the world as well. It's about laying the groundwork for a lifetime of healthy relationships.

So, the next time you find yourself on the verge of a showdown, remember that a little shift in language and tone can pave the way for a more peaceful interaction. You can turn potential battles into opportunities for connection.

## 6.5 Encouraging Responsibility and Independence

Let's say your child is beaming with pride as they successfully tie their own shoes for the first time. It's a moment that fills you with joy and a hint of nostalgia. Encouraging responsibility and independence in our kids is like giving them the keys to their own future. It builds their confidence, allowing them to stride into the world with self-assurance.

Independence enables self-esteem, teaching them that they are capable and competent. When kids feel trusted to handle tasks on their own, they develop a sense of pride in their accomplishments. This lays a strong foundation for their personal growth.

To nurture this independence, start with age-appropriate tasks. For younger children, this might mean letting them dress themselves or put away their toys. Older kids can take on more complex responsibilities, like helping prepare a simple meal or managing their own homework schedule.

The key is to align tasks with their abilities, ensuring they're challenged but not overwhelmed. Setting achievable goals and milestones can also motivate them. Encourage your child to set personal goals, whether it's reading a certain number of books or mastering a new skill. You should celebrate these milestones, no matter how small. You want to reinforce their sense of achievement and encourage further growth.

Balancing support and autonomy is delicate. Think of yourself as a coach, guiding your child through challenges and cheering them on from the sidelines. Offer guidance when needed, but resist the urge to step in and take over.

This might mean letting them struggle through a tricky math problem or solve a social situation on their own. It's about teaching them to problem-solve and think critically. When they succeed, celebrate their accomplishments.

Acknowledge their efforts with a simple high-five or a heartfelt "*Well done!*" These celebrations reinforce their ability to tackle challenges independently and build resilience.

Let's explore how to weave independence into daily life. Start by giving your child choices. Let them decide what to wear in the morning, even if it means mismatched socks and a superhero cape. It's a small step that empowers them to make decisions. Involve them in meal planning or preparation.

Let them pick out a recipe and assist with gathering ingredients or stirring the pot. These activities teach them valuable life skills and show them that their contributions matter. When kids feel involved in family routines, they take pride in their roles. This creates a sense of belonging and responsibility in them.

Embracing independence doesn't mean letting go completely. It's about finding the balance that allows your child to grow while knowing you're there to support them. It's about watching them take their first steps into the world with confidence, knowing they have the tools to succeed.

It is a journey of trust and growth, a partnership between parent and child that strengthens bonds and builds character. As we wrap up this chapter, let's remember that enabling responsibility and independence is just one part of raising a well-rounded child.

You're preparing them for the world, equipping them with the skills and confidence to solve life's challenges. With each step, they become more capable, more confident, and more ready to take on the world.

In the next chapter, we'll explore how to nurture emotional connections. How to ensure that our children feel loved, supported, and understood as they continue to grow and thrive.

# Chapter 7

## *Stress Reduction and Self-Care for Parents*

Assuming you're in the middle of a grocery store, your toddler is attempting their best impression of a banshee. And you have no idea where your car keys are. Your heart races, your palms sweat, and you're convinced everyone's staring. It's in these moments that we could all use a magic button to hit pause.

You should enter deep breathing. This isn't just about filling your lungs. Instead, it's a ticket to instant calm. When you focus on your breath, you're telling your body, *"Hey, it's cool, I got this."*

### 7.1 Practicing Breathing Exercises

It's like a mini-vacation for your nervous system, dialing down the infamous fight-or-flight response. You know the response that loves to make guest appearances at the worst times? Yes, like when your kid decides to turn into a human tsunami.

Deep breathing is your new best friend because it offers immediate physical relaxation. As you inhale deeply, you're not just bringing in air; you're inviting calm into your body. This influx of oxygen slows your heart rate and lowers blood pressure, ushering in a state of tranquility.

With each exhale, you're releasing tension, letting your muscles unwind from the day's stresses. But it's not just about the physical benefits. This practice also enhances emotional regulation.

While focusing on your breath, you gain a moment to step back from the emotional whirlwind. It'll allow you to respond rather than react. In essence, deep breathing helps you find your center, even when the world feels like it's spinning on its axis.

Let's get into some easy-peasy breathing exercises you can try anytime, anywhere. First up is box breathing. Picture a box in your mind. Inhale for four counts, hold for four, exhale for four, and hold again for four. Repeat this cycle a few times. We mentioned this technique in earlier chapters.

It's like hitting the reset button on your brain. Then there's the 4-7-8 technique. Inhale for four counts, hold for seven and exhale slowly for eight. This one's a favorite for winding down before bed.

Both exercises might sound simple, and that's because they are. But don't underestimate their power. These techniques have been shown to quell the storm of stress and bring about a sense of calmness.

Now, here's the secret sauce: consistency. Like any good habit, the more you practice, the better the results. Imagine breathing exercises as your daily dose of calm. Try to do them regularly, and you'll notice a shift. Set reminders on your phone to practice at the same time each day.

Whether it's first thing in the morning, during your lunch break, or right before bed, find a time that works for you and make it a ritual. Consistency is what transforms these exercises from a quick fix into a lifelong tool for managing stress.

Incorporating breathing exercises into your daily routine

doesn't have to be a chore. Think of it as adding a touch of zen to your everyday life. During your morning commute, instead of cursing at the traffic, try a few rounds of box breathing. Turn those red lights into moments of peace.

Perhaps you incorporate it into your evening wind-down. As you tuck the kids into bed and savor those few quiet moments, practice the 4-7-8 technique. It's a gentle way to transition from the chaos of the day to the tranquility of the night.

### The Daily Breathing Tracker

Consider creating a simple chart to track your breathing exercises. List the techniques you try each day and note how you feel afterward. This will help you see patterns and identify which methods work best for you. Tracking your progress can be motivating, and it helps you understand how these practices impact your stress levels.

While weaving these simple exercises into your routine, you'll notice that you're not just finding a moment of peace in the chaos. You're investing in your own well-being. You're creating a ripple effect that can transform both your life and the lives of those around you.

## 7.2 Gratitude Journaling for Daily Positivity

Imagine you're stuck in traffic, the kids are bickering in the backseat, and your favorite song is drowned out by the chaos. It's moments like these when a shift in perspective could be your saving grace. That's where gratitude journaling comes into play. It's not just about counting your blessings but about actively searching for the silver linings amidst the chaos.

When you focus on gratitude, you shift your perspective, and this shift can significantly improve your mood. It's like putting on a pair of glasses that highlights the good and softens the edges of the not-so-great. Gratitude has psychological benefits that are well-documented.

Regularly acknowledging what we're thankful for can increase happiness, reduce stress, and even improve sleep. It's a simple practice with profound effects, helping you cultivate a mindset that sees possibilities rather than problems.

To kickstart your gratitude journaling, consider using prompts to guide your reflections. You can start with something straightforward, like jotting down three things you're grateful for today. It could be as simple as a hot cup of coffee, a moment of laughter with your child, or even just a beautiful sunset you caught a glimpse of.

Another prompt could be to reflect on a positive experience you had this week. This encourages you to relive moments of joy and appreciate them anew. Focusing on these positive aspects helps you train your mind to recognize and savor the good moments, even on the toughest days. These prompts act as a roadmap, steering your thoughts away from daily stressors and towards positivity.

The impact of gratitude on mental well-being is remarkable. When practiced regularly, gratitude journaling enhances emotional resilience. It enables a positive outlook on life, helping you bounce back from setbacks with greater ease. By acknowledging the good, you build a buffer against life's inevitable challenges.

It's like having an emotional safety net that catches you when things get rough. This practice can also improve relationships. Expressing gratitude often leads to a more empathetic and understanding perspective towards others. As you become more attuned to the good, you'll find yourself more patient and compassionate, both with yourself and those around you.

Maintaining a gratitude journaling habit requires a bit of intention, but it doesn't have to be a chore. Try setting a specific time each day for journaling. That way, you're turning it into a ritual you look forward to. Maybe it's in the quiet moments before the kids wake up, or perhaps it's a peaceful end to your day just before bed.

Find a time that fits your schedule and stick to it. Make it enjoyable by choosing a notebook you love or using colorful pens that inspire you. Some parents find it helpful to keep their journals on the bedside table as a visual reminder.

Others prefer going digital. They use apps that prompt them with daily reminders. The key is to make it a part of your routine, like brushing your teeth or having your morning coffee.

### The Gratitude Jar

Consider creating a gratitude jar with your family. Each day, write down something you're grateful for on a slip of paper and drop it into the jar. At the end of the month, gather everyone and read the notes together. It's a beautiful way to share gratitude and reflect on the positive moments you've experienced as a family.

Gratitude journaling isn't more than just practice; it's a mindset shift. When you focus on the good, you transform your outlook, making room for more joy and less stress. It's about finding beauty in the every day, recognizing that even on the most chaotic days, there's something to be thankful for.

In the storm of parenting, these moments of gratitude become anchors. They ground you in positivity and help you navigate the storm with grace.

## 7.3 Creating a Calming Space at Home

Imagine you've just survived another day of work meetings, school pickups, and the never-ending cycle of laundry. Your mind is racing, your body is tired, and all you want is a quiet corner where the world stops spinning for just a moment. This is where a dedicated calming space comes into play.

It's not just a luxury; it's a necessity for mental health. Having a specific area at home where you can decompress is like having an oasis amidst the chaos. It provides a refuge, a place where you can breathe deeply and let go of the day's stresses. A peaceful environment can significantly enhance your mental well-being. It can offer a sanctuary that encourages relaxation and rejuvenation.

When setting up your calming space, consider both **location and ambiance**. Choose a quiet corner or room away from the main areas of noise in the home. It doesn't have to be big. A cozy nook by the window, a small section of your bedroom, or even a transformed closet space can work wonders.

The key is to make it feel separate and unique. Incorporate calming colors and textures to create a soothing atmosphere. Soft hues like blues, greens, or earthy tones can instantly calm the mind.

You can pair these with plush textures – think fluffy cushions, a soft throw blanket, or a comfy rug. These elements engage the senses, promoting a sense of tranquility.

To enhance relaxation, include items that contribute to the calming vibe. Soft lighting is a game-changer. Consider using candles or lamps with warm bulbs to create an inviting glow. The gentle flicker of a candle can be incredibly soothing, almost like a mini spa treatment at home.

Comfortable seating is also crucial. Whether it's a meditation cushion, a bean bag, or a cozy chair, ensure it's something that invites you to sit and stay awhile.

Aromatherapy can deepen the relaxation experience. Essential oils like lavender, chamomile, or eucalyptus can be diffused to create a calming aroma that fills the space. These scents sometimes contain stress-reducing properties.

Incorporating a calming space into your daily routine can work wonders for managing stress. It's your go-to spot for relaxation rituals. You can set aside time each day to unwind in your peaceful corner. Whether it's ten minutes in the morning to set the tone for the day or a quiet evening retreat to reflect and relax, make it a regular practice.

This dedicated time allows you to step away from the chaos and reset, providing a much-needed pause in the whirlwind of daily life. It's a space where you can meditate, read a book, or simply sit in silence, letting your mind wander and your body relax.

The beauty of a calming space lies in its simplicity. It doesn't require grand gestures or elaborate setups. It's about creating a small haven where you can retreat from the world, even if just for a moment.

In a busy household, having this special spot can be a lifeline, providing balance and perspective amidst the craziness. It's a gentle reminder that even on the busiest of days, there's always time to pause and breathe.

## 7.4 Balancing Digital Detox and Family Engagement

It's hard to imagine life without screens, isn't it? They've become woven into the fabric of our daily routines. From the morning news scroll to the late-night Netflix binge. But sometimes, it feels like these devices are no longer just tools. It feels like they're more like demanding little gremlins, constantly vying for our attention. That's where the idea of a digital detox comes in.

It's not about abandoning technology altogether but rather about finding a balance that gives us breathing room. You might not realize it, but reducing screen time can do wonders for your focus and family connections. Without the constant digital noise, you're more present, more engaged, and, quite frankly, more human.

Let's talk about the impact of technology on mental health. We all know that too much screen time can lead to eye strain and sleep disruptions. But it's more than that. It can affect our mood, our relationships, and even our self-esteem.

The endless scroll through social media can leave us feeling less connected, not more. But don't worry, I'm not suggesting you toss your phone into a drawer and forget about it. Instead, consider implementing a digital detox with some simple strategies.

You can start by designating tech-free hours or zones in your home. Maybe it's during dinner or the first hour after everyone gets home. These are golden opportunities for genuine interaction. One where everyone can share their day without screens interrupting.

Encourage tech-free family activities that foster connection. **Do you remember board games**? Or **baking cookies together?** These may sound old-fashioned, but they're fantastic for engaging with each other. If you're feeling adventurous, plan a day hike or a picnic in the park. The goal is to create shared experiences that don't involve pixels and screens.

You might be surprised at how much fun everyone has when the distractions are minimized. Plus, these activities often spark conversations that wouldn't happen if everyone's glued to a device. It's about being present and attentive, both in mind and body. When you're engaged with your family, you want to be physically and emotionally available.

Balancing screen time with family engagement does not mean you have to demonize technology. Instead, it's about using it mindfully. Technology, when used wisely, can actually enhance relationships. Video calls with faraway grandparents, sharing photos with friends, or even watching a family movie together can be bonding experiences.

The trick is to use technology intentionally rather than letting it use you. Set screen time limits for everyone, including yourself. It's easy for those minutes to turn into hours, so having boundaries in place helps keep things in check.

There are apps that track and manage screen usage, offering insights into how much time is spent on different activities. Use these tools to stay aware and make adjustments as needed.

Developing a balanced relationship with technology takes practice, but it's worth the effort. You're looking for that sweet spot where you can enjoy the benefits of technology without letting it overshadow real-world connections. That's what matters most.

By setting these boundaries and fostering tech-free interactions, you're creating a home environment that values connection. It's like carving out space for what truly matters. Things like laughter, conversation, and those little moments that make life truly rich.

## 7.5 Prioritizing Self-Care Without Guilt

Let's face it, self-care often feels like that mythical creature we've heard about but never actually seen. As parents, especially when juggling a career and family, it's easy to let our own needs slide to the bottom of the priority list.

But self-care isn't just a sweet word; it's a key ingredient in maintaining our sanity and improving overall family dynamics. When you take time for yourself, you're not being selfish; you're preventing burnout. Imagine trying to pour from an empty cup. It doesn't work, right? By refilling your own, you have more to give to your family.

Think of it as hitting the reset button, which helps you tackle the day with renewed energy and patience. Finding time for self-care in a jam-packed schedule might seem laughable. But it's not impossible. The trick is to fix it into your routine without feeling like you're adding more to your to-do list.

Short walks can be a game-changer. Even ten minutes around the block can clear your mind and boost your mood. Or maybe it's a quick exercise session – no need for a gym membership. There are plenty of online classes you can squeeze into your day.

If fitness isn't your thing, indulge in a hobby you love. Whether it's painting, knitting, or even baking. These moments of joy are vital in maintaining balance. What's tough is shaking off that nagging guilt that often accompanies the idea of taking time for yourself. But here's the thing: self-care is not indulgent; it's necessary.

Reframe it as an essential part of your well-being, much like eating or sleeping. When you're rested and balanced, you're more present and effective as a parent and partner. Let's flip the script on guilt by acknowledging that taking care of yourself is also taking care of your family. You're modeling positive behaviors for your children, teaching them the importance of self-love and respect.

Now, **how do you protect this precious self-care time?** You can start by setting boundaries. Communicate your needs openly with family members. Let them know that this is your time to recharge, and it's non-negotiable. Maybe it's a Saturday morning yoga class or a Sunday afternoon nap. Whatever it is, be clear about when and how you'll take this time.

Scheduling regular self-care appointments can help cement this commitment. Put it in your calendar, just like you would any other important meeting. Treat it with the same respect, because it's just as crucial.

Encourage your family to support this initiative. Perhaps your partner can take the kids to the park while you enjoy a quiet moment at home. Or maybe your children can help set up a space where you can relax undisturbed.

When everyone's on board, it becomes easier to maintain these boundaries. It's not just about carving out time – it's about creating a culture of respect and understanding within your home.

Incorporating self-care into your life isn't about escaping your responsibilities. It's about equipping yourself to handle them with grace and patience. It's about recognizing that you deserve the same care and attention you give so freely to those you love.

As you prioritize your well-being, you'll discover that you're not just surviving; you're thriving. And that's a gift you give not only to yourself but to your entire family.

# Chapter 8

## *Building Meaningful Family Traditions*

Let's say you're sitting on the couch, surrounded by a sea of toys, laundry, and a faint whiff of yesterday's spaghetti. Your little one is spinning like a top, and you're wondering when your life turned into a live-action version of "*Survivor: Parenthood Edition*."

Amidst the chaos, it's easy to forget the magic of family traditions. But these rituals aren't just the stuff of old movies and holiday commercials. They're the glue that can hold your family together in the whirlwind of everyday life.

### 8.1 Having Regular Family Rituals

Regular family rituals offer a sense of stability and belonging that's as comforting as a warm blanket on a cold night. They provide that emotional security. A predictable rhythm in an often unpredictable world. One that helps both parents and kids feel safe and connected.

Having consistent family rituals is like having a lighthouse guiding you through the foggy sea of daily responsibilities. They offer opportunities for regular bonding, where everyone can drop their worries at the door and gather together. Think of family game nights.

Imagine a table littered with board game pieces, laughter

bouncing off the walls, and a friendly argument about who's cheating at Monopoly. Or maybe it's a Sunday afternoon nature walk, where each step is a chance to breathe deeply.

You all explore and catch up on your week without the distractions of screens or schedules. These moments become anchor points in your calendar, little oases of togetherness where you can all reconnect.

Weekly rituals don't have to be elaborate or time-consuming. They just need to be consistent. Perhaps you rotate themes for game night. One week, it's classic board games; the next, it's charades or trivia. This keeps things fresh and exciting and gives everyone something to look forward to.

It could be a weekly picnic, even if it's just in your backyard or living room, complete with a blanket and sandwiches. The idea is to create a rhythm that fits seamlessly into your diverse schedules. You want to honor each family member's preferences and availability.

These rituals become cherished traditions that everyone anticipates, providing a much-needed respite from the grind. Note that family rituals also play a vital role in reinforcing your values. They're the perfect platform for integrating what your family cares about most into your daily life.

If generosity is a core value, perhaps your family night includes a brief discussion about giving back or planning a small act of kindness for the week. If culture and heritage are necessary, use these rituals to share stories, recipes, or songs from your family's background.

These practices not only uphold what you hold dear but also pass these values down to your children. So fix them into your family's identity. So that as your family grows, so do your rituals. What worked when your kids were toddlers may need tweaking as they become teenagers with packed social calendars.

Be open to adjusting activities as interests shift and schedules change. Involve your kids in the process. Ask for their input on what they enjoy and how traditions can adapt to fit everyone's lives.

Maybe your teenager suggests a movie marathon night, or your little one wants to add a new game to the rotation. Flexibility and compromise are key, allowing these rituals to grow alongside your family and remain relevant.

### How to Design Your Family Ritual

Sketch out a simple plan for a new family ritual. Consider what activities bring joy to your family and how you can incorporate shared values. Write down a few ideas. It could be a weekly craft session, a themed dinner night, or a monthly outing. Involve everyone in the planning process to ensure it reflects your family's unique spirit and interests.

Incorporating new family members, whether they're in-laws, new partners, or even furry friends, can also breathe fresh life into these traditions. Perhaps a new family member introduces a tradition from their past, adding a new layer to your own. Embrace these additions as opportunities for growth, fixing them into your family life.

## 8.2 Seasonal Celebrations and Festivities

Imagine the thrill of the first snowflake as it lazily drifts past your window. Or the vibrant explosion of colors as leaves turn from green to a fiery red and orange. Celebrating seasons together is more than just marking time on the calendar. You're creating a rhythm that punctuates the year with anticipation and joy.

These seasonal festivities build excitement, giving everyone something to look forward to as the months pass. They create a natural rhythm, a beat that keeps the family in step with nature's cycles.

They offer a chance to pause, reflect, and celebrate the small wonders around us. When you weave these celebrations into your family routine, you create vivid memories that grow richer with each passing year.

Spring is a time of renewal, a chance to shake off winter's chill and embrace new beginnings. Consider starting a family garden, where each member gets a small patch to plant and nurture. Picture the kids marveling at the first sprouts, their excitement palpable as they learn the patience and care it takes to grow something from seed.

It's a hands-on lesson in nature and responsibility, wrapped in the excitement of watching life unfold. Fast forward to autumn, when the harvest becomes a reason to gather and give thanks. Host a mini-festival at home with homemade treats, apple cider, and perhaps a pumpkin-carving contest.

It's the perfect excuse to indulge in the cozy comforts of the season while creating something delicious together. As winter blankets the world in white, embrace the solstice with activities like candle-making and storytelling.

Imagine the glow of handmade candles flickering in the dim light as you share tales, both old and new. You all pass stories down like heirlooms, giving warmth to the longest nights.

Cultural and personal traditions add another layer of richness to these celebrations. Maybe your family observes a cultural festival or holiday unique to your heritage. Incorporating these into your seasonal celebrations enriches the experience and also instills a sense of identity and pride in your children.

It's a way of saying, "*This is who we are, and these are the stories we share.*"

Personalizing these celebrations to reflect your family's unique makeup turns them into truly special occasions. Perhaps you create new traditions that blend different cultural backgrounds. Or you introduce a quirky family custom. Something like wearing silly hats at the dinner table that's uniquely yours.

To ensure these festivities are inclusive and enjoyable, tailor activities to engage everyone, from toddlers to grandparents. Think of a buffet of fun where there's a little something for everyone. Age-appropriate activities are key. Young children might enjoy simple crafts or games, while older kids and adults might relish more complex tasks like baking or planning parts of the celebration.

Assign roles to each family member, turning preparation into a shared adventure. One child might be the "*official decorator*," while another manages music or games. This makes everyone feel involved and also enables a sense of ownership and anticipation.

These seasonal celebrations aren't merely about marking the

passage of time. They're an opportunity to strengthen family bonds, to share laughter and stories, and to create a sense of belonging that transcends the ordinary.

They remind us of the beauty in change, the joy in togetherness, and the magic that happens when we gather to celebrate the world around us. As these traditions weave into the fabric of your family life, they become the stories your children will tell. They'll become the memories that will light their way through the changing seasons of their own lives.

## 8.3 Storytelling Nights: Building a Family Legacy

Imagine sitting in a cozy corner of your home, the lights dimmed just enough to cast a warm glow over everyone gathered. The kids are snuggled up in blankets, eyes wide with anticipation, as you begin to weave a tale that's been told for generations. Storytelling is a powerful tradition that's been around since humans first gathered around campfires.

It's not just about the stories themselves, but the shared experience of passing down history, values, and a sense of identity. These narratives are like threads that weave the fabric of family culture, connecting the past with the present. They give your kids a sense of where they come from, anchoring them in a world that's constantly changing.

Creating a space for storytelling doesn't require much. A few cushions, perhaps a quilt or two, and a corner of your living room can transform into the perfect setting. Soft lighting, maybe from a string of fairy lights or a lamp, sets the mood.

You can invite extended family members over, encouraging them to share their own stories. Maybe Grandma has a tale from her childhood or Uncle Joe can recount a family legend that's been slightly exaggerated over the years.

These gatherings become a tapestry of voices and experiences, each contributing to the rich narrative of your family's history. They remind everyone, especially the little ones, that they're part of something bigger, a legacy that's been built over time.

Storytelling is more than just a cozy evening pastime; it's a cornerstone of child development. When children listen to stories, they're not just hearing words. They're expanding their minds. Storytelling enhances creativity as kids visualize scenes and characters in their heads.

It builds language skills, introducing new vocabulary and concepts in a context that's easy to understand. And perhaps most importantly, it fosters emotional intelligence. Through stories, children learn empathy by stepping into the shoes of characters, understanding their motivations, and seeing the world from different perspectives.

Encouraging your kids to create and share their own stories further nurtures these skills. It turns them into confident narrators of their adventures and feelings. Preserving these stories for future generations is an excellent way to ensure that the family legacy continues.

You can consider recording storytelling sessions, capturing not just the stories themselves but the laughter, the gasps of surprise, etc. These recordings become treasures to revisit time and again. Taking it a step further, you might create a family storybook or digital archive. Gather stories from family members, write them down, and pair them with photos or drawings.

It's a project that can grow over time, each new story a fresh chapter in your family's ongoing narrative. This collection becomes a gift for your children, a reminder of their roots and the rich tapestry of tales that make up their heritage.

Storytelling nights are more than just a chance to entertain your kids; they're an opportunity to build a legacy that endures. Through stories, you pass down wisdom, humor, and love. You create a bridge between generations, connecting the past with the present.

You provide your children with a foundation of identity and belonging. These evenings of shared narratives become cherished memories, the kind that your children will carry with them and, one day, share with their own families.

## 8.4 Family Volunteering: Giving Back Together

When schedules never end, finding time to volunteer as a family might seem like adding another task to an already crowded to-do list. But here's the thing: volunteering together can be more than just a feel-good activity. It's a powerful way to teach your kids the value of empathy and community.

When you involve your children in service, you're planting seeds of kindness and social responsibility that will grow as they do. It's not just about helping others. It's about showing your kids that they can make a difference, no matter how small their hands might be. Through shared volunteering experiences, you're contributing to your community and also instilling a sense of purpose and compassion in your little ones.

Finding the right volunteering opportunities can make all the difference. Look for activities that cater to your family's interests and age groups. Maybe your family loves the outdoors. Why not join a local park clean-up event? Armed with gloves and trash bags, you can turn a Saturday morning into a fun and rewarding adventure, teaching your kids to care for the environment.

Or perhaps your clan is more comfortable indoors. Volunteering at a community food bank or shelter can be an eye-opening experience. Sorting donations or serving meals allows your family to connect with those in need. They learn about their struggles and stories. These activities help you give back and gain perspective and gratitude for what you have.

Shared volunteering experiences can do wonders for family bonds. Working together towards a common goal strengthens your sense of unity. Also, creating memories that will last far longer than any Saturday morning cartoon.

It's a chance to see each other in a new light and appreciate the unique contributions each family member brings to the table. More importantly, volunteering can broaden your family's perspective, teaching your children humility and gratitude.

As they interact with people from different walks of life, they learn to value diversity. They also learn to develop a deeper understanding of the world around them. It's a gentle reminder that the world is bigger than just their everyday bubble, and that they have the power to make it a better place.

Integrating volunteering into your family life doesn't have to be daunting. Start by scheduling monthly volunteer days, just like you would a family outing. This regularity ensures that giving back becomes a natural part of your routine rather than something squeezed in when time allows.

It's about making volunteering a meaningful practice that everyone looks forward to. After each volunteering session, take a moment to reflect as a family. Discuss what you learned, how you felt, and what you'd like to do next time.

These conversations are crucial for reinforcing the values you're instilling and for processing the experiences together. It's a chance for your kids to voice their thoughts and ideas and to feel heard and valued.

Volunteering as a family is more than just about helping others. It's a gift you give to each other. It's a way to grow and to nurture a shared sense of purpose. It teaches your children that they can be agents of change.

It teaches kids that their actions matter, and that kindness is a powerful force. As you input volunteering into your family life, you're creating a legacy of service and compassion that will echo through generations.

## 8.5 Creating Annual Family Goals and Reflections

As the new year sneaks in, it's the perfect time to set some annual family goals. You're giving your family a roadmap for the year ahead, complete with pit stops and scenic routes. Goal-setting isn't just for corporate types or personal development junkies. It's a great way to align your family's aspirations and ambitions, ensuring everyone's on the same page.

When you set these goals together, you're creating a shared vision that motivates and directs your family's efforts throughout the year. It's like setting a course for a road trip. Everyone knows where you're headed, and each stop along the way celebrates small victories.

To kick things off, consider holding an annual family meeting. You can grab some snacks, gather everyone around, and let the brainstorming begin. This isn't about setting rigid rules but about dreaming together.

You should encourage each family member to share their hopes and ideas. Whether it's learning a new skill, spending more time outdoors, or planning that elusive family vacation. Once you've got a list, whittle it down to a few key goals that resonate with everyone. A vision board can be a fun tool to visualize these aspirations.

Grab some magazines, scissors, and glue, and create a collage that captures the spirit of your goals. Hang it somewhere visible as a constant reminder of what you're working towards. This visual cue not only keeps the goals front and center but also serves as an ongoing source of inspiration.

Reflection plays a crucial role in achieving these goals. It's easy to set intentions, but looking back is what helps us learn and grow. Throughout the year, take the time to pause and reflect on your progress. Consider creating a family reflection journal where everyone can jot down thoughts, achievements, and challenges.

This isn't just about accountability; it's about celebrating successes and knowing the obstacles you've overcome. As you flip through the pages, you'll see how far you've come and, perhaps more importantly, what you've learned along the way.

Celebrating and documenting progress is just as important as setting the goals themselves. You can host an annual family celebration or retreat to mark the milestones you've achieved. It doesn't have to be grand. A simple picnic in the park or a cozy movie night at home can suffice. The key is to acknowledge the hard work and determination that got you there.

Another idea is to create a "*year in review*" scrapbook or video. Compile photos, snippets of the reflection journal, and mementos from your accomplishments. This tangible record becomes a cherished keepsake, a testament to what your family has achieved together. It serves as a reminder of the power of teamwork and the joy of shared victories.

As we close this chapter on family traditions, remember that these practices are the threads that weave the fabric of your family's life. Whether they're weekly rituals, seasonal celebrations, storytelling nights, volunteering, or annual goals. They provide stability, build connections, etc.

Now, as we turn the page to explore the next chapter, let's consider how these traditions lay the groundwork for solving the challenges of parenting with resilience.

# Chapter 9

## *Dealing with Technology and Screen Time Wisely*

Assume it's a cozy evening, and you're finally settling down with some leftover lasagna, hoping for a moment of peace. But as you glance around, you see your toddler glued to an iPad, your teenager with earbuds permanently affixed, and a game controller where your spouse's hand used to be. Is this familiar?

Welcome to the digital age, where every family member seems to have sprouted an additional appendage. An electronic one. This isn't about banishing screens because, let's face it, they're part of life. But what if, instead, we could manage them in a way that brings balance and harmony to our homes?

### 9.1 Setting Balanced Digital Rules

Setting balanced digital rules might sound like a Herculean task. But it's more like being the conductor of a digital symphony. The key is clear guidelines that everyone understands and respects. When you establish these rules, you're setting boundaries and reducing those oh-so-familiar conflicts over device usage.

Remember the last time you had to pry a tablet from your child's hands? Yeah, me too. By creating a structure for screen time, you'll find that those battles become less frequent and less intense. Plus, when everyone knows what to expect, it's like having a GPS for family tech time. There'll be no more guessing, just clear paths forward.

To start, involve your children in rule-making discussions. Believe it or not, kids have great ideas when you give them a chance to contribute. It's like letting them choose what veggies to eat. They're more likely to comply if they have a hand in the decision. Sit down together and talk about what's essential for your family.

Maybe there are no devices at the dinner table, or perhaps screen time is reserved for after homework. Defining screen-free zones and times gives everyone a break from the digital overwhelm. It also creates opportunities for those meaningful family interactions we all crave.

Consistency is the secret sauce in maintaining respect for these digital rules. Visual reminders or charts can help make the rules clear and easy to follow. You can hang a colorful poster in the living room outlining screen-free hours or use digital tools that remind everyone when it's time to power down.

Consequences for rule breaches should be transparent and fair, like losing screen time for the next day. It's not about punishment but about teaching accountability. When rules are consistent, it reinforces their importance and makes it easier for everyone to follow through.

As your children grow, those digital rules will need some tweaking. A toddler's screen time needs are worlds apart from a teenager's. Regularly revisit these guidelines during family meetings, perhaps once every few months. This ensures the rules stay relevant and also gives everyone a chance to voice their opinions and adjust as needed.

It's like updating a smartphone. You know, trying to keep things running smoothly with the latest info. This flexibility shows your kids that rules aren't static and that their needs and opinions matter as they mature.

### The Family Digital Rules Chart

Create a Family Digital Rules Chart that outlines:

- Each rule
- The reason behind the rules.
- The agreed-upon consequences.

Encourage everyone to add their input and decorate the chart with colors or stickers to make it a collaborative family project.

Navigating technology in today's world requires a bit of finesse, a touch of humor, and a whole lot of patience. By setting balanced digital rules, you're not just managing screen time. You're fostering a home where everyone feels respected and connected, both on and offline.

## 9.2 Educational Apps for Family Learning

Imagine your child's face lighting up with delight as they solve a math puzzle on a colorful app. You can turn learning into an adventure rather than a chore. Educational apps can be the magical key that transforms screen time into a meaningful family experience.

In a world where technology is often seen as a distraction, these digital tools can support your child's education. It can even bring the family closer together. Interactive experiences make learning engaging and fun, turning abstract concepts into tangible skills.

They offer a dynamic way to explore subjects, providing lessons that are as entertaining as they are educational. With the right apps, your child's curiosity can be the driving force behind their learning journey. It can help you participate and share in their excitement.

Now, let's talk about which apps can make that happen. There are countless options out there. However, focusing on high-quality, age-appropriate applications can make all the difference. For language development and literacy, consider apps like:

- "*Epic Ebook Subscription,*" which offers access to thousands of books with features like
- "*Read to me*" is perfect for ages 4 to 12. This app turns reading into an interactive experience, making it an excellent choice for storytime.
- "*DragonBox Numbers*" uses visual numeracy to teach math concepts through playful interactions with characters called Nooms. It's perfect for STEM-focused learning.

It's ideal for ages 4 to 9 and makes math feel like a game rather than a subject to be dreaded. These apps, thoughtfully chosen, can inspire a love for learning that extends beyond the screen.

Integrating educational apps into your daily routine is simpler than you might think. Start by setting time limits for app usage to ensure that screen time remains a balanced part of your child's day. This not only prevents digital fatigue but also encourages your child to savor the time they spend on these educational tools.

Consider establishing structured learning sessions where

siblings can collaborate on app activities. These sessions can enable teamwork and create an environment where learning is a shared adventure.

You might find your children teaching each other new skills, turning education into a family affair. This approach not only reinforces their understanding but also strengthens their bond as they explore and discover together.

Balancing screen-based learning with offline experiences is crucial for a well-rounded education. While apps offer interactive lessons, pairing them with hands-on projects can deepen understanding. It can solidify concepts.

For instance, if your child has been exploring nature through an app like "*Toca Nature*," take them outside for a real-world exploration. Encourage them to observe changes in flora and fauna, connecting digital learning with tangible experiences.

This combination of digital and real-world learning ensures that lessons are retained and applied in meaningful ways. It's about creating a holistic learning environment where screens serve as a tool rather than a substitute for real-life exploration.

Educational apps offer a wealth of opportunities for learning and bonding. You need to choose the right tools and integrate them thoughtfully into your routine. That way, you can transform screen time into a valuable part of your family's educational journey. These apps enhance learning through interactive experiences.

They turn lessons into enjoyable adventures that your children will look forward to. As you explore these digital resources together, you'll discover new ways to engage your children's minds. Ways that build their natural curiosity and create lasting memories of learning and growth.

## 9.3 Scheduling Regular Digital Detox Days

Imagine a world where the only buzzing you hear is from bees in the garden, not from your phone. This is the heart of a digital detox. A dedicated break from technology can work wonders for mental health and family dynamics. In our hyper-connected lives, screens often steal the spotlight, pulling focus from what's truly important.

Digital detox days are like pressing the reset button, giving everyone a much-needed breather from the digital overload. They help improve focus and reduce the mental fatigue that constant notifications and screen time can bring. When everyone steps away from their devices. It's like clearing the fog from a window, allowing you to see and experience life more vividly.

To successfully plan a digital detox, start by selecting a regular day that suits everyone's schedule. Saturdays might be ideal, offering a leisurely pace without the pressure of school or work looming overhead. Planning alternative activities in advance is crucial for success. You're packing a bag for an adventure, so the more prepared you are, the smoother the journey.

Consider organizing an itinerary that includes a mix of activities catering to different interests. This could be anything from cooking a family meal together to exploring a local park. Or even trying out new hobbies. The key is to ensure there's something for everyone, minimizing the temptation to sneak a peek at those screens.

The benefits of tech-free time extend beyond mere distraction. When devices are set aside, family relationships often bloom. It's amazing how much more engaging conversations become when screens aren't competing for attention.

You might find yourself sharing stories, laughing over silly jokes, or discussing those big questions that seem to arise when you're truly present. Unplugging builds a deeper connection. One that allows each family member to be fully engaged with one another. Rather than half-heartedly scrolling through social media while nodding along.

For those looking to add some creativity to their tech-free time, the possibilities are endless. Outdoor adventures, like nature hikes or picnics in the park, provide a breath of fresh air and a change of scenery. There's something magical about swapping the glow of a screen for the warmth of the sun.

If the weather isn't cooperating, consider indoor activities like board game marathons. One where everyone can get competitive in a fun way. Arts and crafts sessions can also be a hit. It allows imaginations to run wild and create tangible memories to cherish. Whether you're painting, building, or simply doodling, these hands-on activities can provide a delightful escape from the digital world.

### Interactive Element: Digital Detox Planner

Create a Digital Detox Planner, a simple chart that outlines activities for the day, ensuring a mix of indoor and outdoor options. Encourage each family member to add their own ideas, making it a collaborative effort. This not only personalizes the experience but also builds anticipation and excitement for the tech-free day.

Incorporating regular digital detox days into your routine can be a transformative experience for your family. It's a chance to unplug, recharge, and reconnect with each other in meaningful ways.

These breaks from technology remind us of the joys of shared experiences and the power of presence. By stepping away from screens, you create space for laughter, discovery, and genuine interactions that strengthen the bonds between you and your loved ones.

## 9.4 Using Technology to Foster Family Connections

Imagine it's a rainy Sunday afternoon, and your crew is scattered around the house. The kids are buried in their devices, and you're debating whether to dive into a new book or catch up on laundry. But then, a **lightbulb moment**. You can use this technology to bring everyone together rather than keep them apart.

Technology doesn't have to be the villain in the family story. When used thoughtfully, it can be a bridge that connects us with our loved ones, both near and far. Virtual family gatherings can transform a mundane evening into a much-anticipated event.

Perhaps it's a game night with relatives who live miles away, where laughter echoes through the screens, and the miles melt away. These digital connections can make the world feel a bit smaller and much cozier.

There are plenty of tools and platforms that encourage this kind of bonding. Video calls are a staple, allowing you to see the smiles and hear the giggles of family members who are miles apart. Platforms like *Zoom* or *FaceTime* are perfect for catching up on life's little moments. Whether it's a birthday celebration or just a lazy Sunday chat, they're cool.

And let's not forget shared playlists on platforms like Spotify, which can set the mood for a family dance-off in the living room. Streaming services offer another way to bond, turning ordinary evenings into movie nights full of popcorn and shared experiences.

Imagine curling up on the couch with your kids, debating which movie to watch. And then, all getting lost in the same story. It's not just about the screen. It's about the shared experience and the memories made.

Balancing digital interactions with face-to-face time is a bit like walking a tightrope. It's tricky but rewarding. Scheduling regular family check-ins can help keep everyone connected, both digitally and in person. It could be a weekly dinner where devices are banned, allowing conversation and connection to take center stage.

It may be a monthly virtual call with grandparents, where everyone gets a turn to share their latest adventures. The key is to make these interactions intentional, ensuring that technology serves as a complement rather than a replacement for in-person time. By setting aside these moments, you create a rhythm of connection that strengthens family bonds.

Setting boundaries for tech use is crucial. It's about ensuring that these digital tools enhance rather than detract from relationships. Establish guidelines for tech use during family meals. Perhaps by creating a simple rule: no phones at the table. This encourages everyone to engage in conversation and listen to each other. This builds a sense of togetherness.

These boundaries are not about restricting freedom but about creating space for connection and communication. When technology is used mindfully, it becomes a powerful tool for bringing families closer. It allows for shared experiences that transcend screens and linger in the heart.

In this digital era, technology can be a friend rather than a foe, offering endless possibilities for family connection. By embracing these tools with intention and creativity, you can turn screen time into family time. One where laughter, stories, and love are shared across distances and generations.

So, the next time you see your family scattered with devices in hand, consider how those very tools can bring you closer together. Start creating moments that matter and memories that last.

## 9.5 Teaching Digital Citizenship and Safety

Let's say your child is happily tapping away on a tablet, diving into a world that seems as vast as the universe itself. As parents, it's easy to feel a mix of pride and worry as they navigate the digital landscape. This is where digital citizenship steps in. Digital citizenship is about being a responsible and respectful participant in the online community.

It's the digital equivalent of teaching your kids to look both ways before crossing the street. In today's digital world, understanding online behavior and safety isn't just important. It's crucial. Teaching your child to be a good digital citizen means showing them how to use technology in a way that is safe, smart, and respectful. You're making sure they know the digital world has rules, just like the real one.

One of the most important aspects of digital citizenship is online safety. This includes teaching children about privacy settings and information sharing. Explain that not everything needs to be shared online, and some information should be kept private. It's like teaching them not to share their home address with strangers.

You can sit down together and explore the privacy settings on their favorite apps. Make it a game to see who can find the most secure setting, turning a potentially dull task into something engaging.

Another critical area is recognizing and avoiding cyberbullying. Talk to your kids about what cyberbullying looks like. It can be anything from mean comments to exclusion from online groups.

Let them know it's okay to speak up if they or someone else is being bullied online.

Encourage them to come to you if they see anything that makes them uncomfortable. The goal is to empower them to stand up against negativity. You want to create a culture of kindness and respect in their online interactions.

As parents, we play a vital role in modeling digital behavior. Kids learn a lot by watching us, so it's essential to show them how to communicate respectfully online. This means practicing what we preach. We should use polite language, avoid unnecessary arguments, and think before posting.

Demonstrating respectful communication sets a positive example. Additionally, practicing mindful tech usage is key. Make a conscious effort to put devices away during family time. You want to show your kids that real-world interactions are just as important as digital ones. It's all about balance.

Creating an open dialogue about digital experiences is another essential component. Encourage regular discussions about what your kids are doing online. Ask them about the games they're playing or the videos they're watching.

Be genuinely interested, and make it clear that they can talk to you about anything they encounter. Address concerns and questions openly. This enables a supportive environment where your child feels comfortable sharing their online experiences.

Regular conversations about technology's role and impact help demystify the digital world. They allow you to guide your child through it, equipping them with the knowledge and skills needed to navigate it safely. This openness also helps you stay informed about the latest trends and potential risks, enabling you to provide better guidance.

In a world where digital interactions are as common as face-to-face ones, teaching digital citizenship and safety is more important than ever. It's about preparing your child to thrive in a growing digital world. You're ensuring they have the confidence and competence to handle whatever comes their way.

This chapter connects the dots between digital safety and the broader picture of family dynamics. By building a strong foundation in digital citizenship, you're helping your child become a responsible and thoughtful member of both their online and offline communities. In the next chapter, we'll explore how to cultivate a supportive parenting community, building networks that enhance and enrich family life.

# Chapter 10

## *Cultivating a Supportive Parenting Community*

Assuming it's Tuesday, and you're staring down another evening of toddler tantrums. And a mountain of laundry that seems to have taken on a life of its own. You think to yourself, *"Is there anyone out there who truly gets this?"* Spoiler alert: there is. And this chapter is all about finding those kindred spirits – your parenting tribe.

Because, let's face it, parenting can feel like a solo expedition through a maze of sleepless nights and projectile peas. But when you connect with like-minded parents, suddenly, the maze has a map, and you're not navigating it alone.

### 10.1 Finding Your Parenting Tribe

Connecting with other parents who share your values and experiences can be like finding an oasis in the desert. It's not just about commiserating over sleepless nights or swapping tips on how to get a toddler to eat something other than chicken nuggets. It's about building a network of support that celebrates the highs and empathizes with the lows.

When you surround yourself with people who understand the unique challenges of parenting, you gain access to a wellspring of emotional support and validation. It's a space where you can share your worries without judgment. One where your parenting triumphs are cheered and where you're reminded that you're doing a fantastic job, even when it doesn't feel like it.

Finding your tribe starts with a willingness to step outside your comfort zone. Remember, nobody's going to knock on your door with a "*Parenting Tribe, Now Forming*" sign. You might start by joining local parenting workshops or classes. These are fantastic venues for meeting other parents who are likely in the same boat as you.

The shared experience of learning about parenting strategies or attending a baby yoga class can be a powerful bonding tool. Attending family-friendly community events is another excellent way to meet like-minded parents. Local libraries, community centers, and even parks often host events where parents and kids can mingle and connect. Bring your kids along. They're instant conversation starters!

The beauty of connecting with a diverse group of parents is the wealth of perspectives it brings. No two parenting journeys are the same, and learning from each other's experiences can be incredibly enriching. Maybe you meet a parent who swears by a bedtime routine that includes a silly dance party. Or someone who has mastered the art of the five-minute tidy-up.

Exposure to different viewpoints can inspire new approaches to challenges you might face. It broadens your parenting toolbox and helps you realize that there's no one-size-fits-all solution. Plus, it's comforting to know that everyone is figuring it out as they go along, just like you.

Once you've found your tribe, nurturing those relationships

is key. Consider organizing regular meet-ups or coffee mornings. These informal gatherings offer a chance to catch up, share stories, and offer support. Whether it's a standing playdate at the park or a monthly dinner at a family-friendly restaurant, consistency helps strengthen these bonds.

Another idea is to create a shared online space for communication. This might be a group chat, a Facebook group, or even a simple email thread. It allows you to stay connected even when life gets busy, and it's a great way to share resources, funny anecdotes, and spur-of-the-moment questions.

### The Tribe Tracker

Consider creating a "Tribe Tracker" to help identify and maintain connections with your parenting tribe. Use a simple spreadsheet or a digital app to record details about the parents you meet. Their names, kids' ages, shared interests, and contact info. This tool can help you keep track of who you've connected with and facilitate follow-ups for future gatherings.

Remember, finding and nurturing your parenting tribe isn't about creating a carbon copy of your own parenting style. It's about embracing the diversity of experiences and insights that each parent brings to the table.

It's about building a community that lifts each other up, offering a shoulder to lean on and a hearty laugh when you need it most. So, go ahead and start reaching out and discover the power of a supportive parenting community.

## 10.2 Engaging in Online Parenting Communities

Imagine you're in your living room, surrounded by toys, dishes in the sink, and a toddler who's decided that naptime is for the weak. You're not alone in this chaos, although it might feel that way. Walk into the digital age, where online parenting communities become a lifeline, offering support and resources when you need them most.

These virtual spaces are like a 24/7 coffee shop filled with parents who get it. You can jump in any time, day or night, to find advice on everything from teething troubles to teen tantrums. With access to a wide range of parenting topics, you'll find discussions on sleep training.

You'll also find discussions on educational activities and even how to cope with the chaos of family life. It's comforting to know that whether you're dealing with diaper disasters or school dilemmas, there's a community out there ready to share wisdom and lend an ear.

The beauty of these online communities lies in their diversity. You're not just connecting with parents from your neighborhood or even your country. You're tapping into a global network of perspectives. It's like opening a window to the world, where you can learn about parenting styles in Sweden or discipline techniques in Japan.

This exposure to global parenting perspectives enriches your own approach. They offer fresh insights and innovative solutions to common challenges. Maybe you'll discover a new bedtime routine from a parent halfway across the globe. Or find solidarity in shared struggles, knowing that parenting trials and triumphs are universal.

Finding reputable online communities can feel a bit like navigating a jungle. With so many options, how do you choose the right one? Start by researching community guidelines and moderation policies. A well-moderated group ensures that discussions remain respectful and supportive.

Look for communities that have clear rules about behavior and privacy, as these are often the spaces where genuine support thrives. Seeking recommendations from trusted sources can also point you in the right direction.

Ask friends or fellow parents about their favorite online groups, or read reviews to gauge the community's vibe. The goal is to find a space where you feel comfortable and valued. One where you're surrounded by parents who share your values and understand your parenting style.

Once you've found your online tribe, participation is key. Lurking might be tempting, especially when you're new, but the real magic happens when you dive into discussions. Share your personal experiences and advice. You might not think you have much to offer, but your insights could be precisely what another parent needs.

Parenting doesn't come with a manual, and sometimes, the best advice comes from those who've been in the trenches themselves. Don't be shy about asking questions or seeking feedback. Whether you're wondering if green poop is normal or searching for tips on sibling rivalry, chances are, someone has been there before and can offer guidance.

But as you engage, remember the importance of maintaining online privacy and security. It's easy to get caught up in the camaraderie and forget about the digital footprint you're leaving behind. Use secure passwords and privacy settings to protect your personal information.

This is your first line of defense against potential breaches. Be cautious about sharing too many personal details, such as your home address or your child's school. It's always better to err on the side of caution. Remember, while these communities are filled with supportive parents, the internet is a vast place. So, it's wise to keep certain information private.

Online parenting communities are a wealth of resources. They offer a sense of connection and camaraderie that can be hard to find in the hustle and bustle of everyday life.

They're a reminder that while parenting can often feel isolating, you're never truly alone. Whether you're sharing triumphs, seeking advice, or just looking for a virtual shoulder to cry on, these digital spaces are there to support you every step of the way.

## 10.3 Creating Local Support Networks for Parents

Let's say it's a sunny Saturday morning, and you're at the local park, coffee in hand. And you're watching your kids tear around the playground like they've just been unleashed. Around you are other parents, laughing, swapping stories, and keeping an eye on their own little whirlwinds. This is more than just a playdate. It's a lifeline.

In-person connections with other parents can be a game changer. They provide immediate assistance, camaraderie, and that all-important sense of belonging. There's something about being able to look another parent in the eye and share a knowing smile that says, "*Yes, I've been there too.*"

Local support networks enable a community spirit, offering easy access to local resources, events, and activities tailored to families. Whether it's discovering a new kids' art class or getting a tip about the best pediatrician in town, these connections are invaluable.

Starting or joining a local parenting group might sound daunting, but it's easier than you think. Begin by organizing a neighborhood parenting group. Start small. Maybe just a handful of parents you know from school or the playground. Set up a casual meeting at a local café or host a potluck at your home.

The aim is to create a welcoming environment where everyone feels comfortable sharing their experiences and insights. If starting a group from scratch isn't your cup of tea, consider joining existing local clubs or organizations.

Many community centers, libraries, and churches offer parenting groups or classes that welcome new members. These established groups provide a ready-made network of support and friendship.

Once you've got your group up and running, maintaining active participation is key to keeping the network vibrant and supportive. Hosting regular meetings or social events is a great way to keep everyone engaged. These gatherings don't have to be elaborate. A simple picnic in the park or a monthly coffee morning can work wonders in strengthening bonds.

To keep things fresh and interesting, consider rotating leadership roles. This not only encourages participation but also brings new ideas and perspectives to the group. By sharing the responsibility, everyone feels invested in the group's success.

Joint activities can also play a significant role in strengthening local networks. Organize group outings to local parks or museums. These excursions provide a fun and relaxed setting for parents and kids to connect. They also offer opportunities for shared experiences and learning. Collaborative projects or volunteer opportunities are another fantastic way to foster connection and support.

Whether it's organizing a neighborhood clean-up or volunteering at a local charity, working together towards a common goal can deepen friendships. It can build a strong sense of community. Plus, they set an excellent example for the kids, teaching them the value of teamwork and giving back.

As we wrap up this chapter, it's clear that building a supportive community is an essential part of navigating the wild ride of parenting. By enabling these connections, you create a network that not only supports you but also enriches your family life.

## Make a Difference with Your Review

*"I heard about this book from a toddler on a trampoline... just kidding!"*

But wouldn't that be something? Imagine kids everywhere chanting, "My Parents are super cool" instead of their favorite superhero's name.

Okay, maybe that's a stretch.

But here's the deal: your review could make that kind of difference for another overworked parent struggling to juggle deadlines and playdates.

Well, they say never judge a book by its cover... I hope people don't do that (and, of course, you didn't as well).

But people indeed judge a book by its reviews, and I totally get it!

Reviews are like little guiding stars for people looking to change their lives. Your review could be the nudge that helps a parent stop scrolling and finally dive into a book that shows them how to balance it all.

You've made it through *The Stress-Free Guide to Positive Parenting*, which means you're well on your way to becoming that parent who balances work, life, and family like a pro. Now, let's help another busy parent who's juggling deadlines and snack requests find the same support.

Imagine what your review could do:

- One more parent finally gets to spend quality time with their kids—without sacrificing work.

- One more family learns that connection doesn't have to mean chaos.
- One more overworked parent realizes they don't have to choose between being successful and being present.

Leaving a review takes less than a minute—quicker than convincing your kid to eat broccoli—and it could guide another swamped parent to the answers they've been searching for. Just visit your recent purchases and share your thoughts.

Your review isn't just feedback—it's a lifeline for someone struggling to juggle it all. Let's show them it's possible to work hard, spend time with their kids, and still feel like a "cool parent."

Rooting for your success, your biggest fan,

Vince Rodgers Lee

# Conclusion

Well, here we are at the end of our journey together, and what a ride it's been! We've tackled everything from toddlers' tantrums to teenagers' tech tantrums, all while trying to maintain a sense of humor and sanity. So, let's take a moment to recap the key points we've covered.

Throughout this book, we've explored various strategies and frameworks, which are your ticket to a calmer, more connected home. They're designed to guide you in:

- Identifying challenges.
- Building mindful habits.
- Enabling emotional connections.
- Continuously refining your routines.

It's about making manageable changes that lead to significant transformations over time. The insights we've shared aren't just about surviving the chaos of parenting. They're about thriving in it. From understanding your parenting style to recognizing emotional triggers, these lessons are essential in navigating the wild ride that is family life.

We also walked through setting clear family goals because, let's face it, knowing where you're headed is half the battle. Establishing mindful habits and nurturing those emotional connections with your kids are game-changers. And remember, reflecting and refining are your secret weapons to keep everything on track.

This book is more than just a collection of strategies. It aims to inspire you to make fundamental changes. The power to transform your family dynamics and your well-being is in your hands. Embrace these mindful parenting practices and watch as they breathe new life into your daily routines.

So, here's the deal: start small. **Implement the strategies in tiny, manageable ways**. Maybe begin with a simple morning routine or a weekly family meeting. The key is consistency and patience. **Rome wasn't built in a day, and neither is a stress-free home**. But with each little step, you're making a lasting impact.

And while you're on this journey, don't go at it alone. Share your experiences with others. Join an online community, connect with a local parenting group, or just chat with fellow parents. There's strength in numbers, and sometimes, just knowing someone else is in the same boat can be a lifesaver.

Take a moment to look back at how far you've come. Celebrate the small wins and those moments of connection that make all the hard work worthwhile. Parenting is a journey filled with ups and downs, but it's also incredibly rewarding. You've got this, and your family is bound to benefit from your efforts.

As the author, I want to thank you for allowing me to be a part of your parenting journey. My passion is helping parents like you create a home environment that is harmonious and fulfilling. I genuinely believe in your ability to make a positive difference for yourself and your family.

So, as you close this book, remember that parenting isn't a

destination but a journey. Each step you take is a testament to your commitment to your family's happiness and success.

Stay hopeful, stay inspired, and most importantly, stay connected with your loved ones. Here's to creating a family life that's not just about getting through the day but genuinely enjoying every moment together. You've got this!

# References


1. Himmat, V., & Kumar, A. (2020). Mindful parenting: A systematic review. Journal of Child and Family Studies, 29(10), 2831–2844.
2. Harnett, P. H., & Dawe, S. (2012). The impact of mindfulness on parenting. Mindfulness, 3(2), 174–183.
3. Baumrind, D. (1991). The influence of parenting style on adolescent competence and substance use. Journal of Early Adolescence, 11(1), 56–95.
4. Hart, K., & Risley, T. R. (1995). Meaningful differences in the everyday experience of young American children. Paul H Brookes Publishing.
5. Webb, L. (2017). Parental self-care: A critical review. Journal of Child and Family Studies, 26(11), 3111–3122.
6. Nelson, J. A., & Burke, R. J. (2000). work and well-being among mothers: A longitudinal study. Journal of Occupational Health Psychology, 5(3), 301–313.
7. Golish, T. D., & Caughlin, J. P. (2002). "I'd rather not talk about it": Adolescents' and young adults' use of topic avoidance. Communication Monographs, 69(2), 133–155.
8. Hart, B., & Risley, T. R. (1995). Meaningful differences in the everyday experience of young American children. Paul H Brookes Publishing.

9. Goleman, D. (1995). Emotional intelligence: Why it can matter more than IQ. Bantam Books.
10. Taylor, G. J., & Bagby, R. M. (2013). Emotional intelligence and its measurement. In J. Ciarrochi & J. D. Meyer (Eds.), Emotional intelligence in everyday life (2nd ed., pp. 43–64). Psychology Press.
11. Hinkley, T., & Taylor, M. (2012). The impact of television on the lives of children. Journal of Applied Developmental Psychology, 33(5), 273–283.
12. Rasmussen, K., & Kuiper, E. (2015). The impact of digital media on children's learning and development. Journal of Educational Multimedia and Hypermedia, 24(1/2), 5–22.
13. Feinberg, M. E. (2003). The internal working models of parenting. In L. Kuczynski (Ed.), Handbook of dynamics in parent-child relations (pp. 91–120). Sage Publications.
14. Pruett, M. K., & DiFonzo, J. H. (2014). Co-parenting and its relationship to child development. In M. E. Lamb (Ed.), The role of the father in child development (5th ed., pp. 313–339). John Wiley & Sons.
15. Mikolajczak, M., & Roskam, I. (2018). A new perspective on parenting: Burnout and its implications. In M. Mikolajczak & I. Roskam (Eds.), Parental burnout: New perspectives for research, practice, and policy (pp. 1–14). Springer International Publishing.
16. Roskam, I., & Mikolajczak, M. (2018). Parental burnout: A multidimensional perspective. In M. Mikolajczak & I. Roskam (Eds.), Parental burnout: New perspectives

for research, practice, and policy (pp. 15–30). Springer International Publishing.

17. Shonkoff, J. P., & Phillips, D. A. (2000). From neurons to neighborhoods: The science of early childhood development. National Academies Press.
18. Webster-Stratton, C. (2018). The incredible years parents, teachers, and children training series: A multifaceted treatment approach for young children with conduct problems. Incredible Years Inc.
19. Hart, K., & Risley, T. R. (1995). Meaningful differences in the everyday experience of young American children. Paul H Brookes Publishing.
20. Baumrind, D. (1991). The influence of parenting style on adolescent competence and substance use. Journal of Early Adolescence, 11(1), 56–95.
21. Kabat-Zinn, J. (2003). Mindfulness-based interventions in context: Past, present, and future. Clinical Psychology: Science and Practice, 10(2), 144–156.
22. Harnett, P. H., & Dawe, S. (2012). The impact of mindfulness on parenting. Mindfulness, 3(2), 174–183.
23. Thompson, R. A. (2016). Emotional regulation and emotional development. Encyclopedia of Cognitive Science, 1–7.
24. Eisenberg, N., Cumberland, A., & Spinrad, T. L. (1998). Social, emotional, and personality development in childhood. In W. Damon, I. E. Sigel, & K. A. Renninger (Eds.), Handbook of child psychology: Vol. 3. Social,

emotional, and personality development (5th ed., pp. 932–1016). John Wiley & Sons.

25. Hill, N. E., & Tyson, D. F. (2009). Parental involvement in middle school: A meta-analytic assessment of the strategies that promote achievement. Developmental Psychology, 45(3), 740–763.
26. Jeynes, W. H. (2007). The relationship between parental involvement and urban secondary school student academic achievement. Education and Urban Society, 39(2), 273–294.
27. Shonkoff, J. P., & Phillips, D. A. (2000). From neurons to neighborhoods: The science of early childhood development. National Academies Press.
28. Webster-Stratton, C. (2018). The incredible years parents, teachers, and children training series: A multifaceted treatment approach for young children with conduct problems. Incredible Years Inc.

9 789334 234817

Printed at Repro India Ltd.